SMUT

SMUT

A SEX INDUSTRY INSIDER

(AND CONCERNED FATHER)

SAYS ENOUGH IS ENOUGH

. . .

GIL REAVILL

SENTINEL

SENTINEL
Published by the Penguin Group
Penguin Group (USA) Inc., 375 Hudson Street, New York, New York 10014, U.S.A. • Penguin Group (Canada), 10 Alcorn Avenue, Toronto, Ontario, Canada M4V 3B2 (a division of Pearson Penguin Canada Inc.) • Penguin Books Ltd, 80 Strand, London WC2R 0RL, England • Penguin Ireland, 25 St. Stephen's Green, Dublin 2, Ireland (a division of Penguin Books Ltd) • Penguin Books Australia Ltd, 250 Camberwell Road, Camberwell, Victoria 3124, Australia (a division of Pearson Australia Group Pty Ltd) • Penguin Books India Pvt Ltd, 11 Community Centre, Panchsheel Park, New Delhi—110 017, India • Penguin Group (NZ), Cnr Airborne and Rosedale Roads, Albany, Auckland, 1310, New Zealand (a division of Pearson New Zealand Ltd) • Penguin Books (South Africa) (Pty) Ltd, 24 Sturdee Avenue, Rosebank, Johannesburg 2196, South Africa

Penguin Books Ltd, Registered Offices:
80 Strand, London WC2R 0RL, England

First published in 2005 by Sentinel,
a member of Penguin Group (USA) Inc.

10 9 8 7 6 5 4 3 2 1

Copyright © Gil Reavill, 2005
All rights reserved

ISBN: 1–59523–012–2

LIBRARY OF CONGRESS CATALOGING-IN-PUBLICATION DATA AVAILABLE

This book is printed on acid-free paper. ∞

Printed in the United States of America

Designed by Carla Bolte • Set in Fairfield, with Akzidenz Grotesque

For Gary and Brian, who understood immediately,

and for Richard, who never will.

In our democracy bad taste has been converted into a marketable, and therefore taxable, and therefore lobbyable commodity.

—WILLIAM FAULKNER

CONTENTS

SMUT

PART ONE

▪ ▪ ▪

FREEDOM FROM EXPRESSION

. . .

THE OLDEST STORY IN THE BOOK

IN NEW YORK CITY IN THE EARLY 1980S, WHEN I FIRST ENTERED into it, the world of commercial sex was tawdry and downscale, a petri dish of percolating microbes and disturbed obsessions.

I loved it.

Then again, I was at that time a twentysomething male, and twentysomething males are such tortured and bizarre anti-exemplars of the human race almost to deserve their very own subspecies.

I was raised in the middle of the Midwest. A few miles from my hometown there's a granite geological survey marker that locates the exact center point of the northern half of the western hemisphere. Middle America precisely. My mother was a kindergarten teacher. My father was a traveling salesman.

Ample enough material against which to rebel, and as soon as I could I hitched up my jeans and hitched on out of there. The country boy coming to the big city is an old story, one of the oldest. I fulfilled the wet-behind-the-ears image in Stevie Wonder's song "Living for the City," where the rube gawks, "New York—skyscrapers and everything!"

Stevie's hero comes to a bad end—he's given a stash of drugs to hold and is arrested. Real life tripped me up in its own special way. After huddling depressed and alone in my spider hole of an apartment for a few months, I stumbled across a want ad in the *Village Voice* that said there was an editorial position open at a "controversial Village weekly." Visions of crusading muckraking journalists dancing in my head, I found myself in the Fourteenth Street offices of Al Goldstein's *Screw* magazine.

I recall very clearly my first exposure to smut, New York style. Like most teenage boys, I had found my way to porn, but in an R-rated sort of way, not an X-rated hard-core way. The first issue of *Screw* I saw that day in 1981 made me feel physically ill. Not a magazine at all, but a tabloid newspaper with ink that smeared off on the reader's hands. The rag's back pages were filled with ads for prostitutes, for which Goldstein charged the same rate as the *New York Times* charged for its advertising. *Screw* fulfilled the basic function of a pimp, procuring customers for hookers.

The front editorial half of *Screw* presented itself as serious redeeming social content: broad-brush sexual satire, witless aggrandizement of publisher Goldstein, and rickety reportage about Manhattan's commercial sex scene. The feature article in the first issue of *Screw* I picked up detailed the phenomenon of "she-male" prostitutes, gender-bending preoperative transsexuals.

I stared at the pathetic publication in my hands. Have I really sunk so low? I didn't react to the sexual content so much as the depressing cheesiness of it, the low-rent stench it gave off. The offices were a shambles, graffiti-scarred, reeking of cigarette smoke. I had always declared my allegiance to what H. G. Wells calls the "jolly coarseness" of life, but there didn't seem much that was jolly here.

Boxes of grainy black-and-white photographic prints, hundreds to a box, were stacked everywhere. It turned out Goldstein bought the porn images that illustrated the articles in *Screw* literally by the pound, like tuna. Dealers in California weighed the boxes of photos before each sale and charged him accordingly. As I waited for my job interview, I took a handful of the shots out of the nearest box and examined them.

The men and women in the photos were none of them model-pretty. They displayed haircuts and fashions from a decade past. Some of them were probably grandparents by now. But here they were, frozen in flagrante forever, entombed in cardboard boxes piled floor to ceiling in the shabby Fourteenth Street offices of *Screw* magazine. My mind conjured up an image of these photos shoveled by pitchfork-loads into the gaping maw of New York's lust.

The dozen or so staff members were all my age, all twentysomethings, attractive, hip New Yorkers, cynical, smart, and funny. Mostly men but a few women, all quite pretty. Talking to them, my initial gut-reaction queasiness began to fade. I suddenly recognized the place. It was a college newspaper, an underground newspaper.

My bohemia. Rejection of the hypocritical, straitlaced, middle-class prudery of my parents' generation. I could live with that.

The editor, a human chimney named Manny Neuhaus, interviewed me through a cloud of Camel smoke, examined my college newspaper clips, and gave me a copy-editing test on which I misspelled the word "tattooed." He said he'd call if they wanted to hire me.

As soon as I left the *Screw* offices, I immediately became depressed again. I crawled back to my cave of an apartment and pulled the covers over my head. This wasn't exactly what I had in mind when I imagined living the New York City dream.

In the next week I got two job offers. One was from a trade magazine called *Floor Covering Weekly*. The other was from *Screw*.

I hesitated. That was the extent of my innocence.

CHAPTER TWO

■ ■ ■

WHAT I'M DOING HERE

THE WORLD HAS CHANGED.

There are three reasons why I wanted to write this book, but that—a changed world—is the first and most important one. Back when I worked in smut (I feel like an old codger, reminiscing in a cracked voice, "Back when I was a boy . . ."), sexually explicit material was fairly well segregated. Those who wanted to consume it had actively to search it out. Since then, the ways in which we can access smut have multiplied staggeringly, exponentially, absurdly, but I still feel strongly that keeping sexually explicit material contained and separate is the right thing to do. I believed in it then, and I believe in it now.

A second reason is that it offends me that so many people who dislike smut are getting it shoved in their faces. This strikes me as a tad undemocratic. No pornographication without representation. It's the cultural equivalent of secondhand smoke. I think adults should be able to use tobacco, just as I am all for adults

7

being able to access sexually explicit material if they want it. But when we get hit with secondhand smoke—or secondhand smut—without being asked, I am offended for myself, I am offended for other people, and I am offended for the children among us.

Third, I don't entertain the same feckless attitude today that I did back then. I have put away the toys of my youth, which included a particular brand of arrogance that delights in offending others. Part of the change is that I became a father. "In dreams begin responsibilities," says the poet Delmore Schwartz, and one of my dreams is that my daughter will grow up in a world that's less trashy than the one I see around me.

I am only getting around now to doing my thinking on a subject that I didn't reflect on much at all, back when I started working in smut. Although I didn't realize it, I had gotten in on the ground floor of a business that would boom and zoom incredibly over the next quarter century, until it would become today one of the largest and most vibrant sectors of the American economy. More people view porn on any given day than watch sports.

If I had applied myself to it in 1981, I could have been a smut millionaire right now, slicing off a piece of a billion-dollar market. But I had seen porn moguls at work, and something inside of me recoiled. I was a complete incompetent as a businessperson. I never aspired to being anything more than a lowly content provider.

The world of smut has become dominant not just monetarily but culturally as well. So I want to talk about my experience in it, perhaps to give some broader indication of what we might be getting ourselves into, maybe to wave a yellow flag of warning.

"Smut" is a word derived from the German, and it means, very simply, "dirt." I use it here knowing that it will open up counter-arguments along the lines of "Sex isn't dirty! Sex is a beautiful, natural part of life."

Sorry, Earth Mother, I'm not talking about human sexuality, the bountiful, mysterious life-enhancing gift. I'm talking about the cheap-thrill onslaught of prime-time television. I'm talking about the dark Satanic porn mills of the Internet.

Sex is like sand on the beach, one thing when it's lying around sparkling in the sun, quite another when it's kicked in your face. When bullies from the media, advertising, and entertainment gang up to kick sex in my face, I say it's smut, and I say to heck with it.

So "smut" means "dirt." The word "decency," on the other hand, is related to the Greek *dekomai,* meaning "I accept." "Indecency," then, can be seen as indicating nonacceptance.

I do not accept.

I do not accept sex as the dominant obsession of our media, entertainment, and advertising. I do not accept being cynically manipulated by sexual images for profit. I do not accept the private sexuality of others invading my public space.

I am a staunch believer in the First Amendment. I am a member of the American Civil Liberties Union. I would never advocate any element of government control of human expression.

The problem is that for a lot of people, the argument ends

there. No law limiting free speech, they parrot over and over, as if that's all there is to say.

But there is a whole boatload of things to say about balance and moderation, about segregating sexual expression from the public commons, about civil discourse and its discontents.

What happens if we agree to the proposition "No government censorship," but still want to talk about changing the kind of world we live in? What happens when we say "No censorship" but still want to continue the conversation?

■ ■ ■

THE UNCHANGEABLE CHANNEL

HOWARD STERN WAS ANGRY. THE SHOCK JOCK HAD JUST BEEN hit with a double whammy—the radio network that carries his morning show, Clear Channel Communications, was fined $495,000 by the Federal Communications Commission, which in turn led Clear Channel to drop Stern from the six network-owned stations that carried him.

How did Stern react? With much spittle-flinging invective on the radio, yes, but also with a grammatically mangled posting on his Web site.

"This is not a surprise," quoth Stern. "This is a follow up to the McCarthy-type 'witch hunt' of the [Bush] administration . . . They . . . are expressing and imposing their opinions and rights to tell us all who and what we may listen to and watch and how we should think about our lives."

What kind of threatened speech was Stern championing?

What particular brand of government-censored expression did this bold First Amendment stalwart defend?

Let's listen in, shall we? If you are squeamish, you might want to avert your eyes.

■ ■ ■

From the official FCC transcript of the *Howard Stern Show*, April 9, 2003, between 7:25 and 7:45 a.m:

> *Stern:* John revealed that in his sex life with his wife they have anal every other time they do it. [Sound of flatulence or anal evacuation] Which seems excessive . . . Jesus H. Christ, just the thought of that [flatulence] obese slob Artie on the bed all sweaty, hairy, and naked giving his girlfriend [flatulence] a, what do you call that, using his mouth in a really dirty place makes we want to friggin' shoot myself.
>
> *Robin:* Oh, my God.
>
> *Stern:* Oh please! So, what, no more anal?
>
> *John:* [flatulence] Let's just say it's every once in a while [flatulence].
>
> *Stern:* But I've heard from your wife [flatulence] that she loves anal.
>
> *John:* Yes, but that's at the dinner table with us, not with the whole world listening [flatulence].
>
> *Another voice, imitating John's mother-in-law:* I saw you telling everyone that you give anal to my daughter. [flatulence]

Odd and incredible as it seems, there are many people, many thinking, caring, intelligent people, who argue that if Howard

Stern is not allowed to rant forth about anal sex on a Wednesday-morning radio show, the Republic will go to hell.

The buttons were already printed. Free Howard. And sure enough, Howard did free himself, by announcing his decision to leave the public airwaves and decamp to satellite radio. Along with the sound of his fans pulling up stakes to follow him, you could hear a collective "good riddance!" also.

I like Howard Stern. I think he can be very funny. But I also like to envision all those people out there who would prefer not to hear about anal sex at 7:25 in the a.m. on their drive to work.

Then they can change the channel.

All right, let's go ahead and change the channel. What do we hear? "Bubba the Love Sponge," speaking on the pleasures of masturbation.

How about turning off the radio?

Okay. I like to be entertained on my morning commute, it takes my mind off the nightmarish traffic, but in the interests of free speech and the First Amendment and an abhorrence of any slight lingering flavor of McCarthyism, I'll switch off the radio.

But wait, what is that up there ahead on the highway billboards? An advertisement for Larry Flynt's Hustler Club? And one for Hooters, and one for Victoria's Secret, and a huge Ralph Lauren underwear ad splashed across the side of a building?

We've entered a hypersex twilight zone.

The 2004 Super Bowl halftime show exposed a lot more than Janet Jackson's breast. It laid bare a fault line in American culture.

Yes, I am a men's magazine insider. I write for magazines such as *Maxim* and *Penthouse*. My message might seem strange coming from someone who is a member of the ACLU. But I'm also the father of a middle-school-age daughter, and the coauthor of a parenting book. In today's pigeonholed reality, that profile might cause distress, like the old robot on *Lost in Space,* which when faced with a logical inconsistency blared, "That does not compute!"

For the past few years I've felt uneasy stirrings that the whole debate over indecency has been skewed, that the free speech I have so long championed has been debased, transformed by a human impulse that turns everything it touches into trash.

I don't think I'm alone in this. If I am going to the barricades for the First Amendment, I don't want to do it in the service of Bubba the Love Sponge. There's a sense that something has been cheapened in American culture, a furtive, largely unspoken shame over the prattling, puerile, priapic obsessions that have saturated every corner of our lives.

Let me say it again, just in case you missed it: I would never advocate any form of officially enforced censorship. If the U.S. government set out to regulate expression, I'm pretty sure it would make a botched job of it. I would hate to have the attorney general declare a national War on Anal-Sex-Talk.

But that said, we have to be able to talk about what kind of culture we are creating, what is good for us as human beings, and what kind of expression might be better left alone. Junk sex might be just as unhealthy (and habit-forming) as junk food. We have to be able to investigate alternatives without somebody shrieking "Censorship!" in our faces.

F. Scott Fitzgerald talks about the true measure of a civilized man being the ability to entertain two contradictory thoughts at the same time. I am a First Amendment absolutist. And I think that today's trash culture is vomit-inducing and has gone too far. (Or Walt Whitman: "Do I contradict myself? Very well, then, I contradict myself!")

Think of it in terms of the owner of a car dealership, who nevertheless believes nine-year-olds should not be allowed to hit the road driving the family SUV. Or a whiskey distiller who draws the line at the idea of a fifteen-year-old getting blind-eyed staggering drunk every weekend.

What's notable about the backlash against the sexual obsessions of contemporary society is that it is being led by people just like me, people who have in the past been intimately involved in creating the kind of cultural expression that is now galloping out of control.

"No one should be able to check out Howard Stern until they're over 16 years old," rapper Chuck D of the group Public Enemy told *New York* magazine in 2004. "I mean, for real. The assumption that children can handle anything is made by people who don't have kids or don't give a damn about them. I don't want the government controlling what I can say, but I know my boundaries."

Another surprise boundary setter:

Once Nasty, Pop Prince Makes Nice

Daily News, April 5, 2004

Maybe Prince really was reading *National Geographic* in the backseat of his "Little Red Corvette."

The supersexy pop legend, who shocked parents with songs about sex and masturbation in the 1980s, says that today's pop culture is way too X-rated for his liking.

"Now there's all these dirty videos," he says. "We're bombarded."

"When I was making sexy tunes, that wasn't all I was doing," he adds in an interview with *Newsweek.* "Back then, the sexiest thing on TV was 'Dynasty,' and if you watch it now, it's like 'The Brady Bunch.'"

After several years of self-imposed obscurity, Prince is back on the charts with a new album and nationwide tour, which includes three shows this summer at Madison Square Garden.

But don't expect Prince, now a practicing Jehovah's Witness, to try to outshock the new generation of lip-locking, nipple-baring, marry-on-the-fly stars.

"My song 'Darling Nikki' was considered porn because I said the word masturbate. Tipper Gore got so mad," he said with a chuckle. "It's so funny now."

Prince, 45, who was out of the limelight because of a feud with record companies, recently was inducted into the Rock and Roll Hall of Fame.

Ever the glam king, he still wears makeup every day and his hair is combed to perfection.

But he also quotes from the Scriptures, mentions Jehovah in his new songs and skips some old fan favorites that are too risqué for his new persona.

"There's certain songs I don't play anymore, just like there's certain words I don't say anymore," he says. "It's not me anymore."

Not a Public Enemy or Prince fan? How about Madonna, a woman roundly criticized in the past for sexualizing the tastes of young people worldwide? Here she is imposing her own version of an FCC fine.

Costly Curses

New York Post, June 3, 2004

The times they have a-changed! Madonna . . . , once known for her lewd behavior as well as her lewd language, has imposed a "cursing fine" on everyone in her tour, including dancers and roadies. "Every time someone curses, they have to pay a fine," said an insider. Liz Rosenberg, Madonna's rep, said: "That is correct—and by the way, she has paid plenty [herself]. I think it is $5 a curse word." Madonna was caught several weeks ago shrieking at her dancers: "Get it right or get the [bleep] out!"—just before she donated to the cursing can.

There are other signs, too, that it is not government interference that will bring change, but voluntary choice prompted by practical (if not ethical) concerns.

Victoria's Secret Calls Off Televised Fashion Show

Chicago Tribune, April 12, 2004

COLUMBUS, OHIO– Victoria's Secret is dropping its nationally televised fashion show this year, at least partly because of criticism following Janet Jackson's breast-baring faux pas at the Super Bowl.

Ed Razek, chief creative officer for the Columbus-based lingerie chain, said Saturday the main reason for the decision was so the company can look at new ways to promote the brand.

Still, he said, "We had to make the decision probably six to eight weeks ago when the heat was on the television networks."

The televised fashion show has generated criticism in the past from groups complaining about supermodels strutting down the runway in skimpy underwear.

Chuck D? Prince? Madonna? Victoria's Secret? What is going on? In twenty-first-century America we have arrived at a place where former provocateurs are now feeling provoked.

Mae West, a woman once jailed for indecency, reacted the same way. "Right now I think censorship is necessary," she said late in life. "The things they're doing and saying in films right now just shouldn't be allowed. There's no dignity anymore and I think that's very important."

There's a natural urge to respond to these folks, "Hey, thanks a whole lot—but why weren't you thinking about that back when you were busy leading us down the garden path?" They are talking about closing the barn door when the horse—the one they freed in the first place!—is already galloping far into the next county. Leaving to the rest of us the task of catching the beast and stabling it once again.

"What is the essence of America?" asks *Parade* columnist and self-identified smarty-pants Marilyn vos Savant. "Finding and maintaining that perfect, delicate balance between freedom 'to' and freedom 'from.'"

In this country, we have been pretty good at protecting freedom of expression. We've failed miserably at establishing freedom from expression.

The discussion about sexual content in today's society—especially in what amounts to its public commons, the region of media and behavior and expression that is open to everyone, young and old, of all beliefs and religions—is extremely divisive. That's because it is a quality-of-life issue that affects the comfort level of everyone.

The irony (and believe me, it's not lost on me, my family, and my friends) is that I come from that world. Since the early 1980s I have worked on and off in what is euphemistically called men's sophisticate publishing, which America knows as porn. For me, familiarity very definitely bred contempt, and I became sick of the repetition, dishonesty, and general overall brain-damaged stupidity of smut.

I have today graduated to being a contributor to one of the leading "men's general interest" magazines in the country, *Maxim,* the difference between that and porn being, in this case, a few strategically placed feathers.

I am thoroughly grounded with all the arguments against limiting, segregating, or censoring this kind of stuff, since I have used those arguments many times myself.

"If you don't like it, don't read it."

"If it offends you, change the channel."

"No one is forcing you to listen."

I am here to tell you that in America at the turn of the millennium, we have created a wholly original phenomenon.

The unchangeable channel.

The "off" switch doesn't work anymore. Our culture has been collectively hotwired.

I am a men's magazine writer, editor, and contributor. And, yes, even one such as I am is here to tell you that enough is enough.

■ ■ ■

CHAPTER FOUR

CULTURE-WHIPPED

LET ME SKETCH OUT A DAY I SPENT WITH MY MIDDLE-SCHOOL-AGE daughter. It started with an episode of a "tween" sitcom—that is, a show targeted for kids between the ages of nine and twelve. I passed through the room where my daughter was watching the program and just happened to catch a scene where twin seven-year-old girls tried out a new cheerleading routine they were practicing.

"Shake it, shake it, shake it," the seven-year-olds squeaked, sticking out their fannies, slapping them, and then reacting as if they'd just touched a hot stove.

I looked at my daughter, who gazed at the tube with the vacant-eyed look that is, if statistics about TV watching are right, the most common facial expression in America. I felt upset at the clear sexualization of a pair of prepubescent girls, and especially annoyed that their antics were played for laughs.

"Shake it, shake it, shake it," chanted the seven-year-olds.

Ha, ha, ha, went the laugh track.

"How cute" was the barely subliminal message being conveyed to my daughter. "Look at these tykes acting like a pair of pole dancers!"

Real funny, I posed my unspoken thought against the canned laughter. But I resisted the impulse to point out the inappropriateness of the message. Just the day before, my daughter and I had talked about a Ludacris song she liked, about thuggin' and clubbin' and ho's (street slang for "whores"), and I didn't want to come off as constantly preaching.

In present-day America, we learn to swallow many of our responses to modern culture, so as not to appear prudish, vanilla, or outré.

A commercial interrupted the seven-year-old lap dancers. A trailer for *The Girl Next Door,* the latest theatrical movie from Fox about to open. "I want to see that," my daughter said.

I let that pass, too. The movie is rated R, and my daughter is not allowed to see R-rated movies. The plot involves a porn star moving in next door to a teenage boy.

Why are they advertising an R-rated movie on a program aimed at twelve-year-olds? That was my thought, but again I said nothing out loud.

We got into the car for a drive, my wife up front next to me, my daughter in back with her beloved iBook laptop. She had just received the computer as a present for her birthday and had already downloaded seventy-five songs into her iTunes jukebox. She sang along as the iBook trolled automatically through her playlist.

My wife and I were talking, not really paying much attention to what was going on in the backseat, when I heard my daughter mouthing the words to D12's hit "My Band," featuring Eminem (who was born Marshall Mathers) as lead rapper.

"I swear to f****n' God," my twelve-year-old sang, "Dude, you f****n' rock! Please, Marshall, please, let me s**k your c**k."

"What was that?" I asked, twisting my head around and almost running off the road. In our household, which is not a free-speech zone, we have well-articulated boundaries about what sort of words are inappropriate. "You don't even know what that means!"

"I do, too!" my daughter responded, even though I know she doesn't, and she knows I know she doesn't. It turned out she had downloaded "My Band" from the Internet, where there was a choice of the cleaned-up "radio" version (which she is allowed) and the unbleeped explicit version (which she is not allowed). My wife and I fell asleep at the switch, not monitoring which version our daughter actually chose.

But what happened next we could not have stopped or avoided through any action of our own. We drove into Manhattan along the West Side Highway, through a commercial district of warehouses and garages. The carriage horses that operate in Central Park are stabled here, and across the highway the military museum installed in the decommissioned aircraft carrier USS *Intrepid* looms massively on the docks.

Also located in this neighborhood, so that it acts like something of a portal to all of New York City, is Larry Flynt's Hustler

Club, a sprawling burlesque house situated in a former automobile showroom. Flynt adorns the side of the building with a billboard-sized sign showing a woman, her mouth pursed, blowing on her hand.

I glanced back at my daughter, who was gazing out the window, keeping an eye out as she always does, for a glimpse of the carriage horses. What she got instead was a teasing display of adult sexuality. I didn't say anything, but I tried to imagine what was passing through her mind.

She had asked about the club before. "What's that?" How to explain a strip joint to your pre-teenage daughter? Keep it simple, my wife always advised, when communicating grown-up concepts to children. "Some men like to watch women dance," I had told her, back when she first asked about it.

Even for someone such as myself, with experience in the world of commercial sex, the explanation sounded lame and incomplete. I recall suddenly feeling unworthy of the charge of being a parent. How could I unravel the tangle of politics, morality, exploitation and hedonism that represents the knotted sexuality of America today? I had trouble explaining it to myself, much less to my daughter.

That specific day was not atypical. My family has been treated to X-rated movies on the DVD screens of cars in the lanes next to us. The Howard Stern radio show has boomed out of what seemed like nuclear-powered car stereo speakers when we were attempting to enjoy a morning in a riverside park.

Now as I watched her gazing out at Larry Flynt's smut emporium, I realized the degree to which we have failed our children.

In a political sense, the young are powerless, voiceless, totally reliant on adults. In myriad important ways, in providing them with health insurance and legal protection, our record as a society is spotty at best.

But we also have left unfulfilled our function as guardians of their cultural environment. The boundaries of their world have been repeatedly breached, many times by people interested in making money and dismissive of all other considerations. All too often, our children are exposed to the loud, frenzied, garish spectacle of adult sexuality. They get their faces rubbed in it.

So within the course of one hour of one very ordinary day, I had been treated to a vision of twin seven-year-old fanny slappers, a sex professional taking up neighborhood residence, and groupies begging for oral sex.

I didn't like it. It made me mad.

What had happened to my family that day was that we had been "culture-whipped," a term that measures the gulf between the expectations of the viewer (or listener) and the content of the media. When you whip your head around, asking "What was that?" not believing your eyes and ears, you've been culture-whipped.

In today's media climate, whether we want it or not, we are inundated, saturated, beaten over the head with sex. Television, our national public commons, has an ever-mounting percentage of explicit sexual content on cable, shading down to the mere leering double entrendre and snickering innuendo of broadcast sitcoms. It's difficult to find a program that doesn't reference sex.

It's egregious, it's out of control, it's too much. Media, advertising art, and entertainment constantly shove images at me that I am just not interested in seeing.

The average child in America puts in a full workweek, forty hours, consuming media. That means our kids are getting a snootful of this stuff, all day every day, week in and week out.

I am reminded of Groucho Marx, who once had a guest on his interview program *You Bet Your Life,* a woman who said she had nine children and that she and her husband liked it.

"I like my cigar," Groucho responded, "but I take it out of my mouth every once in a while."

In today's culture, the "cigar" of smut has been permanently and surgically stapled to our lips. We can't take it out of our mouths at all, much less every once in a while.

■ ■ ■

CHAPTER FIVE

THE CLOWN PRINCE

WORKING AS AL GOLDSTEIN'S GHOSTWRITER IN THE EARLY 1980S, I became well acquainted with the man who was called the clown prince of pornography.

Little known outside of New York City (a fact that frustrated him endlessly), Goldstein was a local celebrity due to his cable-access TV show. He was consistently mentioned in gossip columns like the *New York Post*'s "Page Six." The Rupert Murdoch–owned *Post,* normally bedrock conservative, liked Goldstein for his entertainment value.

Liz Smith, doyenne of New York's gossip columnists, also liked Goldstein, and mentioned him repeatedly in her columns, always using approving terms. He was named a "Voice of New York," in *New York* magazine's twenty-fifth anniversary issue. He was friendly with celebrities like Bill Cosby, who lived on Goldstein's block on the Upper East Side.

That was Goldstein, the public figure. Meanwhile, I was get-

ting to know the private Goldstein. Although he could be gener-
ous and funny, he was quite a bit harder to take in the flesh than
his gossip-pages persona might imply. All his humanity seemed
to have been stripped away, reducing him to a single attribute—
appetite.

He was all mouth. He ate, sucked, consumed, inhaled.

I recall Bogart in the movie *Key Largo*. "What do you want,
Rico?"

And the crime boss Edgar G. Robinson as Rico says, "I want
more!"

Goldstein wanted more. He would sit in his tchotchke-
cluttered office and shop mail-order catalogs compulsively, ripping though their pages and circling item after item.

"I want that!" he would call to his beleaguered secretary. "Get
me that!" His two most well-worn phrases. One after another, he
would buy and discard an endless spew of gadgets, clothes,
watches, jewelry, and geegaws, in thrall to an unattractive, unsat-
isfiable urge to devour.

He was diet-maddened the whole time I knew him, and bal-
looned up and down in girth like a blowfish. Watching him eat
was a poor exchange for his always picking up the check. He resembled a massive, squalling, undiapered infant, always scream-
ing to be fed something—new food, new toys, new sensations.

More.

He treated other humans as a toddler does. Either you fed his
needs or you were deemed by his infantile mind to be some form
of competition. He screamed and bellowed at his secretaries, of-

ten reducing them to tears. His friendship was nearly as toxic as his hatred. His life was a chronicle of burned bridges and scorched-earth relationships. One of his secretaries had him hauled into court for harassment. One of his ex-wives also charged him with harassment. Goldstein's only child refused to invite his father to ceremonies when he graduated law school.

I was a not-so-innocent bystander to some of this. Goldstein never trained his volcanic anger on me, I guess because I did a good job for him. But I always wanted to take aside the Liz Smiths of the world, the Bill Cosbys and the rest of Goldstein's adoring fans, and say, "Don't you see? This man is a monster. He hurts everyone he comes in contact with, and has no other principle other than ultimate selfishness."

As a publisher, Goldstein had intellectual pretensions, but they were laughable, and I rarely saw him read anything longer than a magazine article. In his own writing (as opposed to my writing for him), he was master of the mixed metaphor. One example that sticks in my memory is his mention of a movie plot that was "cheese-like in its complexity."

I eventually came to understand that there were two Goldsteins: Goldstein the symbol, and Goldstein the man. Goldstein the symbol was the one lionized by the media, held up as a paragon by *New York* magazine, treated as hot copy in the gossip columns. Look at how liberal and enlightened we are, went the unspoken message, we take seriously even a vile pornographer.

Rhetorically, of course, Goldstein had extremely pronounced principles, the foremost being the First Amendment and free speech. I was hired to articulate these principles for him. In effect, I was his spin doctor, taking the gross reality of Goldstein and spinning it into public relations gold.

As a struggling twentysomething writer, I was all too easily suckered in. Defending free speech? Wow! In the pretzel logic of my imagination, the fat slob who sat chomping a cigar in editorial meetings was an important crusader for the First Amendment. I was doing important, groundbreaking work.

But gradually I recognized that Goldstein was an ultimate opportunist, selfishly using free-speech guarantees to satisfy his appetites. In Utah there was once a porn emporium called the First Amendment Bookstore. Goldstein embodied precisely that level of cynicism.

Yes, Goldstein talked a good line about free speech. He was a killer in televised debates, heaping abuse on his opponents as prudes, puritans, and rubes. But it was all a sham. He was ultimately dismissive about everything, including the U.S. Constitution.

I kept a journal for some of the time I was with him, and paging through it now, I can pick out Goldstein quotes that I scribbled down, such as this one: "[Bleep] the government and [bleep] the Bill of Rights—I wipe my [bleepin' bleep] with the Bill of Rights." As I got to know him, it became abundantly clear that Goldstein couldn't have cared less about the First Amendment, or about anyone's freedom but his own.

One reason why Goldstein was so well known in New York was his *Midnight Blue* TV show, which was on public-access cable back in the early 1980s. The program, a showcase for him, comprised little more than his rantings, his reviews of X-rated films, and his interviews with porn personalities. But the whole hour-long fiasco was dominated by endless ads for call girl agencies.

Midnight Blue was the bane of Manhattan Cable, which was owned back then by the giant media conglomerate Time-Life, Inc. (precursor to today's Time Warner). More accurately, Goldstein himself was the bane of Manhattan Cable, since he was constantly harassing the company, complaining about the transmission of his show, sparring over censorship issues. He reviled Time-Life, cursing its corporate officers regularly on his show.

"I just watched this incredibly bloody horror film on Manhattan Cable," he said to me one day, gloating. "It was really violent, and it was shown in prime time. I think we can really stick it to them."

He directed me to pen an opinion piece in his name for the *New York Times'* op-ed page, excoriating Time-Life for distribution of violent programming.

I knew Goldstein well. I knew he did not care at all about violent programming. He didn't care about the effects such programming might have on children. All he cared about was sticking it to his avowed enemy, Manhattan Cable.

Yeah, right, I remember thinking, leaving Goldstein's office that day. Like the *New York Times* is going to let a porn mogul attack Time-Life on its editorial pages. But I went ahead and wrote the piece. I didn't think much about it back then. It was a goof. I was a hired gun. I approached the whole thing as an exercise in rhetoric.

To my surprise and Goldstein's extreme satisfaction, the

Times did indeed allow the *Midnight Blue* producer to attack Time-Life.

I tell this story neither to portray Goldstein in a sad light (although this was the light that shone throughout his life, permeating it like a bad smell) nor to attempt a point about mainstream American corporations and their collusion in the porn world. I just want to quote part of what I wrote back then at Goldstein's behest:

"Gore-nography"

New York Times op-ed page, June 3, 1984

> . . . HBO and Cinemax, owned by such a bulwark of American business as Time-Life, Inc., are doing more damage to the ideals of innocence and childhood than the most radical fringes of the pornography industry . . . It is hard to think of a TV executive so insulated, so removed from the imperatives of ordinary existence as to consider violent films suitable for children . . . "Midnight Blue," my own cable TV show, is clearly unsuitable for children, but it is not intended for them and is scheduled, as its name implies, after midnight. And perhaps it is a bit ironic for a man in my position to dictate morals to HBO, Time-Life and the house that Luce built. But clearly, if we are to protect our children, something must be done.

This wasn't really Goldstein. This was me channeling Goldstein. He gave me the subject and the slant, and left the word choice up to me.

So maybe I haven't changed all that much since the days I worked in smut. Because I still stand by the words I put into Goldstein's mouth back then.

I don't care what kind of tripe you produce. I don't care if you feature porn stars, Mother Teresa, or Martin Boorman on your show. Curse, cuss, sputter all the obscenity you want.

But keep it out of my face. Keep it where my kid won't encounter it. Have the civility to grant me a choice about whether or not I want to watch it. Schedule it after midnight, where it belongs.

CHAPTER SIX

■ ■ ■

WASTING AWAY IN POTTERSVILLE

"THE POT CALLING THE KETTLE BLACK" IS A SAYING THAT HAS ITS equivalent in every language, pointing to a fundamental recognizable human truth. The original is from *Don Quixote*: "Said the pot to kettle, get away black face." Shakespeare had his own version: "The raven chides blackness."

Why should you listen to a men's mag professional, a writer whose disposable prose has customarily been published pages from (if not opposite to) lavish full-color spreads of female flesh?

Because I know whereof I speak. I know the strategies, the self-justifications, the arguments that the purveyors of sexual content use. As I said, I have voiced them myself.

It's not so much that I have had a change of heart, or that I am trying to redeem myself for my sordid past.

The problem is that all the champions of free expression are fighting an old battle. They are convinced they have joined a long tradition of courageously standing up against the censors, against the Mrs. Grundies, the bowdlerizers, the Comstockian enemies of free speech.

But we've moved on. Boy, have we moved on. It's not an "anything goes" culture; it's an "everything must go everywhere all the time" culture.

Yes, for a long time I was in the thick of the men's magazine industry. I ghostwrote articles for Al Goldstein in *Playboy, Penthouse,* the *Los Angeles Times,* the *New York Times.* Through him I met or worked for Hugh Hefner, Bob Guccione, and Larry Flynt. I helped edit a one-shot special porn-parody magazine called *Sluts and Slobs,* now a cult favorite worth hundreds of dollars on eBay.

I didn't think anything of it. Or, more to the point, I didn't think.

Then my wife and I had a daughter.

Little by little, my view of the contemporary social landscape changed. In the last two decades, since the time I first got a job at an X-rated newspaper, porn has increasingly seeped into the mainstream. Bondage gear I once knew as the exclusive purlieu of fringe fetishists is currently available at suburban malls.

Meanwhile, within the liberal stockade, where so many media workhorses have corralled themselves, any objection to the pervasiveness of sexual content is met with whinnies of outrage. The First Amendment stalwarts run on outdated tapes, imagining themselves to be sticking up for the poor victimized James Joyce in his battle to get *Ulysses* published in the United States, or a martyred Lenny Bruce and his right to curse in nightclubs. Alternately, as with Howard Stern, they label themselves victims of McCarthyism.

I would like to ask you to imagine another kind of victim. My friend Don runs his own swimming-pool service in a suburb of Phoenix. He has two young children and a wife he loves. He is not particularly well off, but he gets by and enjoys life. Politically, he would land left of center on pretty much any scale you might apply.

But talking with him, I always find Don deeply uneasy about the current cultural atmosphere. He often speaks longingly of "getting out," finding a cabin somewhere and living a back-to-the-land life with his family.

He's not a prude, he's not a fundamentalist. He's just an ordinary guy trying to give a good life to his children.

And he's angry and upset at the kind of stuff he is forced to swallow whenever he turns on the television, drives in a car with the radio on, or goes to the movies.

He's angry and upset, and sometimes I catch him a little sad, too. That out of all possible worlds we could have created, this is the one we've settled on. Out of the great and groovy achievements we could have accomplished, it has all come down to *The Swan,* porn pop, and Bubba the Love Sponge.

Ugh.

"You know what this country reminds me of?" Don asks. "You know that scene in *It's a Wonderful Life,* where George Bailey is running down Main Street in Bedford Falls—"

"Pottersville," I correct him. I know where he is going with this.

"Right," Don says. "It's Pottersville, because this is when George Bailey was never born, so he gets to look and see how things turned out without him. And he's running down Main Street, and it's all neon and bars and strip joints and stuff like that. That's the kind of country we have right now. We're living in the version of reality where George Bailey was never born."

Quite a few people share Don's sense of loss. We're sad as hell and we're not going to take it anymore.

A lot of times Don blames me. I used to trot out my First Amendment arguments to him. I don't do that much anymore, but he's still throwing them back at me.

"I always think of you out there in New York writing for your magazines," he told me. "I wonder if you ever think of me out here in the boonies, just trying to do the right thing."

It's not about free speech. It's about choice.

My friend Don doesn't really have a choice about the kind of world he lives in. The overheated, reverse-puritanical, trivialized sexuality of twenty-first-century America is forever being shoved down his throat. And that has made him increasingly frustrated. He's not as glamorous a cause as, say, James Joyce or Vladimir Nabokov, or even U-2's Bono. But I think there are a lot of people out there like him.

A Kaiser Family Foundation poll conducted in summer 2004 found that 60 percent of parents feel uncomfortable ("concerned," "very disturbed") about the levels of exposure their children get to sex in the media. Six of ten. Let's call them the Disturbed Six-in-Tenners. Don is one of them, and so am I. That's an incredible poll result, if you think about it. All across

America, there is widespread frustration about the nasty turn our culture has taken. That frustration is matched with widespread paralysis over how to respond.

Widespread frustration, widespread paralysis.

In the early 1980s a sculptor named Richard Serra installed one of his massive steel creations in the middle of a public plaza in lower Manhattan. *Tilted Arc* was a 120-foot slab of rusted steel that sliced through a public square where many office workers crossed every day. Because of the sculpture, they had to go a couple hundred yards farther to reach their destinations.

The office workers complained.

The defenders of artistic expression rose up in defense of *Tilted Arc,* visions of a battle against the Philistines dancing in their heads. Serra himself took a dismissive attitude—I was commissioned, he essentially said, and there it is. If you don't like it you must be a bourgeois boob.

Even back then, the arrogance of the argument enraged me. Here is some clerk just trying to plod through his workday, and some other guy drops a huge load of artistic expression in his path.

That's what I feel about the arguments (the nonarguments, really) of those who turn back every suggestion of moderation by rehashing their defense of the First Amendment. Please, I want to tell these stalwarts, there are people out there who are just trying to get through their Super Bowl without a breast being shoved in their faces.

The response is automatic, a counterargument that essentially can be refined to a single word: "Tough." Tough you don't like the way things are going, tough you are offended, tough you worry about your children.

I was speaking to a literary agent friend of mine, a former editor at a big New York publishing house. We were talking about Janet Jackson at Super Bowl XXXV.

"I want more breasts on television, not fewer," she said. It was an airy, deliberately contrarian comment. I don't know how much it reflects the truth or was just rhetoric, since I don't know if she is concerned about the amount of nudity her young daughter sees on television.

But it reflects the dismissive attitude toward all the people who *are* concerned, and who considered the Janet Jackson stunt an affront.

Tough, say the free speech stalwarts. There should be more of this stuff, not less. Screw the Super Bowl audience, screw the office workers, screw the working stiff just trying to get through his day.

My rights trump yours.

Jack Heidenry, a coworker of mine on magazines from *Hot Talk* to *Maxim* who now works at *The Week*, the national news-digest magazine, responded with an angry e-mail when he learned I was working on this book. "What's disappointing," Heidenry wrote, "is not that you've become a no-holds-barred controversialist, but just another suburban dad."

All right, I thought, reading the e-mail from Jack. Maybe I am flattering myself to consider my pro-reticence stance to be controversial. You're right, Jack.

Then I mulled over that phrase "just another suburban dad."

At first I swallowed it as an insult, because after all I *am* just another suburban dad. But the more I thought about it, the more I realized the phrase typified a certain attitude left over from cultural wars of a previous epoch.

Bourgeois, suburban, family—bad. Demimonde, urban bohemia, free spirit—good. My dear friend Heidenry, who has written one well-received book-length history of the sexual revolution and another well-received book-length history of *Reader's Digest,* could be excused if he has visions of manning the barricades against prudery.

But Jack Heidenry himself has at various times in his life qualified as a suburban dad. Don from Phoenix is a suburban dad. Truth of it is, suburban dads are the backbone of the country. They do all the boring déclassé stuff like paying their bills and raising their children and going to work. There's no reason for them to catch it in the Bermuda shorts just for being who they are.

That's arrogance, that's elitism, that's something that my friend Don in Phoenix and everyone else who thinks things have gone too far shouldn't have to put up with.

If you are like me, you tend to block a lot of smut-ridden modern society out, from an impulse of self-preservation if nothing else.

But I'd like to take you on an unblinking guided tour of Pottersville, U.S.A., to see what kind of culture we have wrought in America at the opening of the third millennium. The obvious place to start, of course, is with the single form of media that most dominates our lives.

PART TWO

■ ■ ■

POTTERSVILLE, U.S.A.

Hold back the edges of your gowns, Ladies,

we are going through hell.

—WILLIAM CARLOS WILLIAMS

■ ■ ■

CHAPTER SEVEN

THE BOOB TUBE

PRIME-TIME TV

THE PUBLIC COMMONS IS AN ANCIENT CONCEPT, CARRIED OVER from British law, establishing land that all members of the community share. The idea has taken some jolts over the centuries, what with the old-fashioned village square (usually organized around the town hall) devolving into the local shopping mall. But as a real and valuable ideal, the commons remains central to our status as social animals.

For all of us, for society as a whole and for each individual and family in it, the first and foremost public space in our lives is not the mall or the town square or the nearest interstate highway. What represents the grandest, most accessible, most populated public space in our world today?

For a long time now, America's public commons has been television.

At a climactic moment in *Wuthering Heights* (both the book

43

and the movie), Cathy, the heroine, says about her obsessive identification with the hero, "I am Heathcliff!"

The average American, especially the average American child, can say that without hesitation about television. "I am TV!" Viewing peaks at around age twelve at a whopping seven hours a day. In terms of taking up an average child's time, TV is ranked above school and family, below only sleep.

Television is a mirror. What we are doing, when we sit slack-jawed on the couch (sci-fi writer Ray Bradbury calls TV "a Medusa which freezes a billion people to stone every night"), is watching a version of ourselves.

But if it's a mirror, it's a crazy fun-house mirror. And the single aspect of our lives that TV most distorts is sex.

Due to exhaustive research from the nation's too-much-time-on-their-hands academics, we know fairly accurately how our side of the fun-house mirror—the "real" side—deals with and thinks about sex. The rate of extramarital sex, for example, on this side of the mirror, is low, with only a tiny fraction of adults confessing to having an affair within the past year. An overwhelming majority of us are monogamous. More people are abstemious (having no sex) than are gay.

We generally don't place sex at the center of our lives, we don't unduly obsess about it to the exclusion of other aspects of existence, we don't even make it a particularly dominant theme in our social interactions. For most of us, it's part of life, not life in itself.

But let your gaze stray for a moment into the fun-house mirror of television.

"Honey, look," says the resident ditz of one of the most profitable shows on TV, as she picks up a latex glove. "This is the strangest looking condom I've ever seen. Why, what an oddly shaped penis the doctor must have."

That's a laugh line from *Will and Grace*. We have passed into the world of all sex, all the time. Specifically, we're watching an episode of the half-hour sitcom that aired at eight o'clock on a summer Thursday. The ditz is Karen, portrayed by Megan Mullally.

A few beats later, the same episode, the same character: "Doctor, since I have you here, true or false? Milk, milk [indicating her breasts], lemonade [indicating her crotch], and around the corner fudge is made?"

And how about this colloquy, between a doctor, a nurse, and the main character, Will, played by Eric McCormack:

Nurse: Here you go doctor, your instruments have been lubed and sterilized—and so have I.

Will: Hey, Nurse Sheila. You were once my nurse at the sperm clinic.

Nurse: Hmm. I'm not so good with faces. Drop your pants, I'll see if it rings a bell.

Doctor: Thanks for bringing these over so fast.

Nurse: I could do it slower next time.

Doctor: No, I like it fast.

Nurse: I'll bet you do.

Doctor: Mmm-hmm.

Nurse: I like a guy with a little meat on his bones.

Doctor: More cushion for the pushin'?

Nurse: Hey, you said it.

The nurse gives a playful slap to the doctor's butt as she exits. "If she weren't my sister," the doctor says to Will and Karen, "I'd be tapping that ass big-time."

In what kind of world do you make ribald repartee with your sibling? If I spoke like that to my sister, I'd probably earn at least a quizzical look, maybe a corrective slap in the face. Who talks to each other in this way? Perhaps someone does, somewhere, since it's a big sprawling world out there. But it's not the sort of routine most of us find natural or familiar.

Okay. This could be an anomaly in more ways than one—in our own lives as everyday humans, and in the life of the show itself. In the interest of fairness, let's skip through the schedule to springtime, when a young man's fancy turns to et cetera, and check in with *Will and Grace* once more.

The show kicks off with Karen again, waking from a dream, and having Jack assure her, apropos of nothing, that wet dreams are common among young boys. Jack himself describes a dream about movie star Jude Law, leering about having seen "the long arm of the Law."

Meanwhile, Will and Grace launch into a real estate business deal, which Jack labels a "new version of having sex with each other." Their main rivals are a lesbian couple. As a business tactic, Will decides to the seduce one of the lesbians, while the other turns the tables on him and attempts to seduce Grace.

Hilarity ensues—or at least, what passes for hilarity on a prime-time sitcom. Will, ostensibly searching for a condom, blunders into Grace and the lesbian realtor dancing. You and she? Her and her? Me and you?

If you find yourself grinning at this quick thumbnail of the plot, you probably have a more prominent funny bone than I— but of course, it must lose something in the telling. With a laugh track, with actors hamming it up, it can be nothing but the finest that TV has to offer, since the show has been nominated for forty-nine Emmys and has won twelve.

I recognize the humor. Oh, boy, do I. We used the exact same latex glove gag in the pages of a porn magazine I used to work for, although we did it in an explicit cartoon. Back then it was simply an example of puerile, sexually explicit humor, in a place that you'd pretty much expect puerile, sexually explicit humor— *Screw* magazine. Not available to minors. Sold only to adults who went out of their way to purchase it. Not thrown in the face of any and all who happened to be flipping through channels.

And two couples, mistakenly attempting each other's seduction? Why, that's Shakespeare, isn't it? Well, yeah, it is, but this stuff bears the same relation to the Bard as a mud pie to the Empire State Building.

That's about the octave where the humor of *Will and Grace* is pitched, to the tune of porn mags and mud pies. Since the show appears in the eight o'clock time period, which the networks soberly recognize as "family hour," porn mags and mud pies are what families are getting.

Will and Grace is rated TV-14. The show gained a lot of its popularity from being scheduled immediately after the insanely popular *Friends.* Much of the carryover audience from *Friends,* it must be said, consisted of children, adolescents, and young adults—many of them well under the recommended minimum age of fourteen.

There's a moronic monotone to the gags on *Will and Grace* that reminds me of when I was a child, when my sisters and I used to laugh uproariously over the word "bottom." This level of humor is not cataclysmic, it won't bring down the Republic, but *Will and Grace* is a prime example of television's obsession with sex.

I like my cigar, but I take it out of my mouth every once in a while. On *Will and Grace,* the stogie never strays from smack dab in the middle of the show's leering, wink-wink-nudge-nudge mug.

"All television is children's television," states author Richard Adler, which can mean either of two things, both true—that children wind up watching all kinds of television, or that all television is childish. Placing it in a slightly different perspective, former FCC commissioner Nicholas Johnson writes, "All television is educational television. The question is, what is it teaching?"

Will and Grace teaches a weak-willed, ungraceful lesson, demeaning, silly, and profane. Through the looking glass there exists a race of humans with spectacularly one-track minds. The source of their appeal is our adolescent anxieties over sex. In the face of these absurdly monomaniacal creatures, our only choice is to titter nervously.

Let's flip the channel, move a network over to CBS, and switch genres. *Cold Case* is a forensic police show of the kind that dominate the ratings (though *Cold Case* itself earns only average numbers of viewers). This also is a family-hour show, a particular rerun episode that aired at 8:00 p.m. on a summer Sunday.

Detective Lilly Rush must investigate a murder in her former neighborhood, which a fellow detective describes as "hooker land." A local church organist named Mitch Bayes was found dead in the back of his van in an area of town known for drugs and prostitutes. A blond prostitute Detective Rush interviews explains that, because of the AIDS epidemic, she performs only oral sex for her customers.

Other details of the crime emerge. The victim's son and his friend admit to using the large stack of porn magazines that police found in the van. The son also says he has used the van to solicit prostitutes in the same neighborhood where his father was found dead.

Hookers, porn, and murder.

Splendid family fare, CBS!

At the *Cold Case* episode's climax we are treated to an explicit replay of the murder, which was actually committed by the victim's wife in revenge for an extramarital affair. This was difficult for me to watch, and would be totally unsuitable for my middle-school-age daughter.

Two networks, two nights in summer, two family hours. What have we learned?

Comedy = sex.

Drama = sex.

A change of season, another crop of shows, but the same old story. The effort to keep smut off the public airwaves in the wake of the Janet Jackson controversy quickly fizzled out. The networks mounted fall shows that were positively moronic in their obsession with sex. On ABC's *Desperate Housewives,* actress Eva Longoria's character has an affair with a seventeen-year-old landscaper. ABC also broadcast the teen soap *Life As We Know It,* perhaps the most egregiously sexualized show ever aimed at a young audience.

I am offended by the impoverishment of imagination here, by the absolute paucity of creativity. Sure, I don't want my daughter peering into this looking-glass world and concluding that this is how things are done in real life. But I also don't want her seeing the world through such a narrowing lens. It's as though Gutenberg's printing press were used strictly to print comic books. I like comic books. But I like other kinds of books, too.

Yes, television is very educational, as Groucho Marx used to say. Whenever someone turns it on, I go into another room and read a book.

Who owns the airwaves over which this smut is broadcast? I'd be willing to bet that if you asked a hundred people that question, not many would come up with the correct answer.

We do.

Actually, the Pew Research Center once did indeed ask a similar survey question in 2002, and came up with disheartening results. Less than a third of the people polled knew that CBS, NBC, and ABC don't own the frequencies on which they broadcast, that they are merely licensed (for free) to use those frequencies. These networks, and others, such as Fox, WB, and UPN, serve at the public's discretion.

Public ownership of the airwaves makes good sense. What we

are talking about, in effect, is the air, the atmosphere, very literally the public space we all share. It's our world, and the networks just borrow it. No single corporate entity should own the public commons. CBS shouldn't own it, and it doesn't. And yet the networks act very much as though they do, as though they have some sort of proprietary claim on the airwaves.

The networks, of course, aren't all that interested in folks pondering the question. Don't look *in* the media for a lot of exposés *about* the media. The public ownership–private licensing of the airwaves isn't an arrangement that is going to warrant a lot of mention on television. The networks would rather leave us in the dark.

It's as if a traveling salesman knocked on our door, offering us a deal: let me have the free use of something that you own, which I will use to make myself rich, and I will do things with your property that you might not agree with and that might harm your family and lead your children astray.

No one in their right mind would sign on the dotted line. Even though that is precisely the deal that the networks have offered us, it is rarely presented in such stark and realistic terms. The junk that is zinging through the atmosphere at fifty-four megahertz is by all rights our junk, and the networks are using our public space to deliver it.

But oddly enough there is an instance where three-quarters of the American public (85 percent if you count in satellite dishes) have signed on the dotted line for a slightly different entertainment contract, not in the automatic, unknowing way we sign up for broadcast television, but by making a direct and quite conscious decision to bring cable television into their homes.

■ ■ ■

"THE ID ON THE GRID"

BASIC CABLE

LEGALLY, CABLE IS A QUITE ANOTHER BEAST FROM BROADCAST television. Unless we happen to have stock in Cablevision or Adelphia or Comcast, we the public do not own the physical grid of wires over which cable is carried, the way we own the airwaves that broadcast television uses. Government, usually local government, might franchise this or that cable system to operate in a given community, but that is very different from the licensing of a public broadcasting frequency to a private company. The FCC has only limited say over cable.

So doesn't the choice of cable represent a gigantic vote of confidence in the content of television? When virtually everyone in the United States pays to pump it into their homes, doesn't that mean the American people endorse what Hollywood and the networks are delivering up? It's all about choice, isn't it?

Let's take a look at what kind of choices basic cable offers us. Cable networks such as Comedy Central, FX, Oxygen, A&E,

and MTV, many of them owned by large media corporations, schedule numerous exclusive programs and episodic series. How do these programs compare with the offerings of broadcast television for sexual content?

Immediately, it becomes clear that we are once again marooned in the land of the fun-house mirror. Once again, we are looking at a place where the focus on sex is almost obsessive. While the frequency of sexual reference might be about the same as in broadcast television, the crudeness and junkiness of the content is much more egregious.

Sometimes, intentionally so. *South Park,* Comedy Central's notorious animated show, is precisely engineered to push every button of anyone who finds explicit sex, foul language, and amoral outrageousness offensive. That's the whole reason for the show. There's a French phrase, *épater les bourgeois,* which translates roughly as "tweak the middle class." That's the motto of *South Park.*

The few times I've watched the program, I've enjoyed it. I laughed at it. Prepackaged transgression can be very funny, especially since *South Park* doesn't really challenge any fundamental social beliefs. But I won't let my daughter watch it, and I wouldn't ever want to have it force-fed to me if I wasn't in the mood.

I found the irreverent logic behind *South Park* to be fairly transparent—and readily familiar from my years of working in smut. What Trey Parker and Matt Stone, the gents behind *South Park,* are really saying with all their nose-tweaking is that they have a horror of appearing middle-class themselves. They are aghast at the thought of joining the hordes of workaday folk in banal, humdrum lives.

The style of humor in *South Park,* which makes fun of such ordinary folks relentlessly, helps calm Parker and Stone's fears that they might really be those ordinary kind of people. Parker and Stone were raised in screamingly middle-class environs. Their parents included a geologist, an insurance broker, a home-maker, and an economist. Parker's hometown is a South Park–like suburb of Denver called Conifer. Stone was raised in Littleton, the Denver suburb on which South Park is based. There's noth-ing quite like acting out the rejection of your origins on national television.

We all want to picture ourselves as cooler, more knowing, bet-ter than the everyday schmuck in the streets. *South Park* finds an audience (it's one of the most popular shows on basic cable) not only because it is witty but also because its message strokes our sense of cultural insecurity. See, you're not a boob, the show whispers to us, you're not an unsophisticated rube like the ones we make fun of, and the ones you are laughing at. You're special, just like the millions of the people who are watching *South Park* along with you. Every one of them is special, too.

The problem with *South Park* is the same problem with Joe Camel, R. J. Reynolds's cartoon corporate mascot who used to pitch cigarettes. Animation naturally draws the attention of chil-dren who were weaned on a steady diet of cartoons. My daugh-ter is lured by the animated images of *South Park,* but then betrayed by the program's bait-and-switch strategy. Think it's a kiddie show? Surprise, it's not!

South Park is a cartoon show about children ostensibly aimed at adults. The animation is intentionally crude, to highlight the joke. In some sense it taps into a show that Art Linkletter (and later, Bill Cosby) used to host, *Kids Say the Darnedest Things.* It's funny, because it is surprising, to hear adult words come out of a child's mouth.

A single episode of *South Park* contained 160 uses of the un-bleeped word "shit."

"Don't mind Kyle, everyone," ran a recent line in the show, "he's just got a little sand in his vagina."

South Park contains the seeds of its own destruction. The more children imitate what they hear on *South Park* (and under-twelve viewership of the show measures in the millions), the less surprising it will be to hear kids curse. It will be matter of fact. And then *South Park* humor won't be funny anymore. Take away *South Park*'s humor, and the show is just sad.

Comedy Central also features less accomplished, more prattling sexual humor than that used on *South Park.* The network's short-running satire, Parker and Stone's *That's My Bush!,* featured this faux interview with the First Lady:

Q: You mean you haven't made love since you moved to the White House?

A: No, no, we still make love. You know, there are different kinds of sex.

Q: Oh, the president's not going downtown anymore, huh? Did he used to go downtown?

A: Like a champ. It's why I married him.

On *The Man Show,* a determinedly down-market, *Maxim*-like take on frat-boy humor, cameras followed original hosts Jimmy Kimmel and Adam Carolla to a fertility clinic on a quest to discover which one of the them had the highest sperm count. Referring to his ejaculate, Carolla says, "Mine's going to come out with such a thrust, Jimmy, it's going to suck my underpants up my ass."

Nor is Comedy Central the only cable network to exploit sex as an entertainment staple. On A&E's *100 Centre Street,* a law drama, characters toss off random lines such as these: "You know what love is, do you? Could you shoot me a beaver?" On *The Real World,* a reality show on MTV, a male recounts a threesome with two women: "I took a backseat and watched the two of them do a little spanky-sucky."

Basic cable represents a "channel" that is indeed changeable, in that you can elect not to invite it into your home (although you may risk your children being treated as social outcasts by their peers). The high degree of acceptance that cable has managed to gain is perhaps in spite of its sexual content, not because of it. One media critic described the high sexual content of cable television as "the id on the grid." Cable content producers should not be so quick to pat themselves on the back, since the widespread opinion about their product is best summed up by the Bruce Springsteen song "57 Channels (and Nothin' On)."

■ ■ ■

TRUE LIES

REALITY TV

BUT WAIT A MINUTE. ISN'T ONE OF THE MOST PROMINENT RECENT trends in television (broadcast and cable both) the switch from sitcoms to reality programming? That's not fun-house-mirror stuff, is it? That is just us, real, live, breathing human beings. Reality TV just shows reality, right?

A full fifth of network programming nowadays is reality based. But we're a long way from Allen Funt and *Candid Camera*.

"We're sitting in [bleeping] traffic, you know, miles from where we're supposed to [bleeping] turn. Is there a [bleeping] reason why we're just cruising this [bleeping] thing? If not, let me out at the [bleeping] hotel. We're supposed to go to the [bleeping] Palms, and we're driving just down the [bleeping] Strip on a Saturday [bleeping] night, no [bleeping] reason? [Bleep] get to the [bleeping] place. The Palms Hotel is back [bleeping] that way. How the [bleeping] can you [bleeping] not know how to get to a [bleeping] hotel? [Bleep!] . . . Turn that [bleeping] camera off, before I throw it out the [bleeping] window."

Ah, yes, reality. But there are a lot of realities, about a quarter billion of them in the United States alone, last time I checked. Which one is this? Or, more to the point, whose reality is this?

We are out of the family hour now, but barely, since the episode of the WB network's *The Surreal Life* from which that spew was lifted aired in the nine-o'clock time slot on an early-winter evening. The speaker was Vince Neil, lead singer of the off-again on-again heavy metal band Mötley Crüe (which used to boast of its output as "music to crash your car to," with Neil indeed getting into a deadly auto accident while DUI, killing a friend of his).

The Surreal Life delights in featuring celebrities of the entertainment firmament whose stars have dimmed, collapsed, and become red dwarfs, if not black holes. Vince Neil has since concluded that his appearance on *The Surreal Life* was a mistake that may have harmed his career trajectory. So that's whose reality we've checked into, as if into a mental health asylum—a singer from a heavy metal band who thinks the show is too low-brow for his high standards.

That was just the first season.

The second season of WB's *The Surreal Life* actually featured a porn star, a man I've met a couple of times and found a genial enough moron, Ron Jeremy. Even in the world of smut, he was roundly ridiculed as a loathsome physical specimen, nicknamed "the Hedgehog" for his hirsute physique. I like Ron. I find it hard to look at him, but I like him. I probably like a lot of people who shouldn't necessarily gain access to the bully pulpit of a national television show.

Apart from his porn-performing duties (he's been in over four thousand sex videos) Jeremy styles himself a stand-up comic, and I've seen that act, too—about which I can only say Ron Jeremy has a talent for humor in the same way he has a face for radio. On *The Surreal Life* episode that aired on a Sunday night in winter, Jeremy was paired with such stellar talent as Rob Van Winkle, a.k.a. Vanilla Ice, and Tammy Faye Messner, the former TV evangelist perhaps better known as Tammy Faye Bakker.

Here's a just a taste:

Tammy Faye: "I own an organ that used to be in Frank Sinatra's house in Palm Springs."

Ron Jeremy: "I own an organ that was in many, many movies."

Ahhh . . . ha-ha-ha!

Vanilla Ice moons the audience, Jeremy and former *C.H.I.P.S.* lead actor Erik Estrada verbally compare penile endowment, and a woman flashes her breasts at the camera.

A month later, another episode of *The Surreal Life* featured a barbecue to which Ron Jeremy invited his associates from the world of porn video. Their moment basking in the sun of national TV! Their fifteen minutes! The pornsters appeared dazed, like deer in the headlights. Grinning, celebrity-struck deer. I recognized many of them. All good-natured, well-meaning folk who happen to make their living having sex. Given my checkered career, I certainly can't hold that against them. I just wonder what they were doing in prime time.

Under Jeremy's urging, the whole show degenerated into a topless flash-fest, centering on who was going to expose whom.

"Traci would have shown me her breast," whines Ron about Traci Bingham, a former performer on *Baywatch*. He evinced disappointment when Bingham's fiancé showed up and she abruptly switched gears to become "innocent and sweet" (as Jeremy put it).

"One of the ladies propositioned me," confides Estrada to the camera. "She wanted to give me an oral compliment."

Cut to the woman herself: "Wanna come outside for a blow job?"

Not much is real in *The Surreal Life*. It's fake. In fact, it's not surreal, either—somewhere, Salvador Dalí, Man Ray, and the rest of the surrealists are spinning in their graves.

Lest you think I'm picking on *The Surreal Life,* there are numberless other reality programs that, while not quite as crass and porn-oriented, succeed in lowering the bar to the point where anyone with any taste at all will bark their shins on it.

"Good taste is the enemy of creativity," said Picasso, but it turns out that bad taste, too, can pretty well cripple the human imagination.

On UPN's *America's Next Top Model,* we are privy to a bikini-waxing session with the contestants. "There are only two people who have been down there," says one contestant, Robin, as an attendant works on her nether region, "myself and my gynecologist, and I give him crap." In the background, shrieks and cries of pain as the hot wax cools and then is ripped off, along with the contestant's pubic hair. On another episode, one of the contestants explains her irritability by saying she is "surfing the crimson wave right now," adding that "I just don't need this kind of [bleeped 's**t']."

In another *Top Model* episode, we listen in to Elyse, a contestant, ripping into her rivals: "Robin, how [bleeped 'f***ing'] dare you show me that 'Foolish is the atheist' Bible verse this morning and ask me what do I think of it. What the [bleeped 'f**k'] am I supposed to think of it? You know what I think of you? Foolish is the woman who believes that [bleeped 'g*ddamn'] tripe. Giselle, you [bleeped 'f***ing'] worthless [bleeped 'c**t']. You are so wasteful, bitchy, stupid. You're worthless. Your parents must be ashamed of you. Jay, you offended me today. I know that medical school is hard work. It takes a [bleeped 'f***ing'] ass to cover every [bleeped 'f***ing'] place. Damn it, let me [bleeped 'f***ing'] die. You bitches."

When contestants are not sufficiently foul or racy for prime time, producers are not above injecting a dose of outright unreality into a reality show. On the first season of Fox's *Joe Millionaire*, aired on a Monday night in the nine o'clock time slot, Evan and Sarah disappear into the woods together. Captions pop up: "Smack," "Slurp," "Think it'll go better lying down?" But when the episode aired, Evan and Sarah both confessed to the press that no actual sex had taken place.

Again and again, porn is a central theme of reality TV. "Do you like watching porn?" Errol asks Lisa on CBS's *Cupid,* which aired at nine o'clock on a Wednesday night in summer.

"I like watching porn," Lisa says.

"When we get married, we can make our own movie," Errol says.

An invitation such as this would send most of the female population bolting from the room, but on reality TV, it's just business as usual. There have been instances of off-camera oral sex on Fox's *Mr. Personality* (complete with zipper-lowering sound effects), partially pixellated male strippers on *The Surreal Life,* and this exchange between a suitor and his prospective mother-in-law on the first season of NBC's *Meet My Folks:*

> *Bride-to-be:* "Jason likes to be spanked."
> *Jason himself, confessing:* "I like to be spanked."
> *Rhonda (the mom):* "You're making me have this vision of my daughter spanking your butt."

One of the pioneers of the reality TV craze was MTV's *The Real World,* which debuted in 1992 and set the relentlessly sexual tone for imitators to follow. But MTV is such a massive presence in our children's lives, and such a prime purveyor of smut, that it deserves a chapter all its own.

∎ ∎ ∎

I DON'T WANT MY MTV

MUSIC VIDEOS

IN THE AFTERMATH OF JANET JACKSON'S STUNT-FLASHING OF one billion viewers at the Super Bowl XXXV halftime show, a healthy segment of the American public was furious. This fury was, as the psychologists say, "overdetermined," meaning it was caused by much more than a five-second glimpse of a thirty-seven-year-old woman's breast.

We had, all of us, been there before, culture-whipped by explicit sexual images when we least expected them and didn't particularly want to see them. That Super Bowl halftime show was just the trigger. The anger had been building for a long time.

Jackson resembles many entertainers in that she is addicted to a curious celebrity cocktail, narcissism laced with hubris. Her performance that evening was founded on the quite mistaken assumption that I (sitting out there with a billion others in worldwide TV land) desired nothing more than to ogle her naked flesh. That I along with the rest of humanity found her so overwhelmingly sexy we couldn't wait to see her strip. I don't know how to let you down easy about this, Janet, but mine is a very definite vote of "No, thanks." (Janet herself always claimed that the exposure was inadvertent.)

I used to have a friend who thought it was funny to be rude to strippers. While the rest of audience was catcalling, "Take it all off!" he would be drunkenly shouting, "Put it back on!"

Most of the reaction to the Super Bowl show focused in on Janet Jackson's nipple-baring, but I for one found at least as troubling the dirty dancing that MTV saw fit to gift us with. Actually, it went quite a bit beyond dirty dancing. It was more like obscene dancing. Again, the mistaken assumption: you will find our indecency irresistible.

"I was told that's how young people dance today."

That was a comment of Sumner Redstone, CEO of Viacom, the second largest (behind Time Warner) multinational media conglomerate in the world. He was responding to audience reaction against the halftime dirty dancing. Viacom owns MTV, which means that Redstone is more or less responsible for the mess at Super Bowl XXXV.

But in fact he's not responsible at all, if we are to take his comment at face value. In the wake of the show and the resulting furor, Redstone's equivocation hung in my mind. He was "told"? By whom? His minions? As if that explained it.

"I was told that's how young people dance today." For some reason the line irked me beyond all perspective. These were the words of a cowardly and evasive man, unworthy of running a company that provides us with so much of our entertainment.

The buck stops over there, with my minions, or with the young people who dance that way. The buck certainly doesn't stop with doddering old Sumner Redstone, who is "told" things about "young people."

All right, Sumner Redstone, allow me to tell you something about young people today. One reason that the rage for dirty dancing has swept the land is that a channel directly under your control popularized it. MTV has relentlessly sexualized music and all other aspects of adolescence in America. If hypersexuality is a virus, MTV is patient zero, the source and initiator of the plague.

The dirtiest secret about MTV is that its viewership skews young. There are literally millions of twelve- and thirteen-year-olds watching the channel. Just when many adolescents poke their heads out of the protective shell of the family for the first time, tentatively feeling their way in the world, learning values and how to act, what greets them? The profane, ugly, and relentless sexual assault of MTV. It amounts to a cultural rape.

And Sumner Redstone, the man responsible, is "told" that it's what young people enjoy. Pedophiles argue that their victims enjoy their ministrations, too.

MTV is rife with this pass-the-buck attitude. After the Super Bowl debacle, MTV president Judy McGrath characterized the show as "exciting" and "great," and said that it was tarnished only by "five seconds none of us knew anything about."

Play dumb. Like Sergeant Schulz on *Hogan's Heroes*—"I know nuthink!" Janet was an aberration. It was all a mistake, "a wardrobe malfunction." Ignore the dirty dancing and fellow performer Nelly, with his soft-core "Hot in Here" antics. Ignore the fact that this style of material is bread-and-butter for MTV.

At the time, MTV officials felt the heat and vowed they would do the "responsible" thing, scheduling sexually graphic music videos only at night. Britney Spears's aptly named "Toxic" video, in which the singer is trapped in fishnet fashions, writhing for the delectation of male admirers, was one of the spots exiled to nighttime rotation.

How long did MTV's "responsible" policies last? Not even a month. Then it was back to form, back, I guess, to MTV's irresponsible policies. "Toxic" returned to daytime rotation before February 2004 was over. And who did an MTV spokesperson blame when taken to task by a TV critic?

"We decided to take a temperature check, we listened to the audience, we wanted to make sure we still felt good about the images on MTV. The audience," the spokesperson declared to a *New York Daily News* writer, "decided they wanted to see these artists."

See how that works? It's the audience, not the grand poohbahs of MTV (and certainly not Sumner Redstone), that is responsible for content.

MTV has very respectable social service campaigns on voter registration and sex education. Unfortunately, the channel's obsessive focus on sex gives you the idea that it's all just window dressing, designed to give otherwise indecent content some socially redeeming camouflage. And incredible as it seems, the channel also enforces some standards on music video content.

There's a "no bondage" rule, for example. Sexual intercourse implied or explicit is outlawed.

That ought to surprise viewers who've watched MTV, because there don't appear to be any standards in play here at all. In music videos such as "Toxic," sex is a brand of martial arts, with the crotch a prime weapon. The unrelenting sexism of the whole enterprise is depressing. I recognize these images, these dynamics, these contexts from my years in porn.

At times the connection is quite literal. *Porn to Rock,* a series on MTV's sister channel VH1, helped boost the media profile of porn star (and author of *How to Make Love Like a Porn Star*) Jenna Jameson, among others. Lil Jon and the Eastside Boyz, an MTV favorite, starred in and produced their own porn video in 2003. We haven't come that far since the days of MTV's *Andy Dick Show,* which featured a segment called "Anus and Andy." According to the Parents Television Council, the skit portrayed an anus puppet defecating and comic Andy Dick eating the excrement.

Sumner Redstone would no doubt say that this is just the way kids watch TV today. MTV presents a porn-like landscape to our children, acclimatizing them to the realm of pimps and ho's, softening them up for when they will be able to enter the real world of hard-core.

■ ■ ■

TANGLED IN THE WEB

INTERNET SEX

IF TELEVISION IS DRENCHED IN SEX, THEN AMERICA'S OTHER technological public commons, the Internet, is equally saturated with it.

In one sense, this should have been expected. Sexually explicit content has always been in the vanguard of new media technology. When photography was developed (so to speak) in the mid-1800s, the "French postcard" represented its initial widespread commercial distribution. The first commercial movie clip showed a (then-racy) kiss.

Likewise, in the video revolution of the 1970s, the new technology was driven at the start by a single market—the raincoat crowd. The first videocassette recorders were massive things, the size of steamer trunks. An overwhelming percentage of the first commercially available videos were X-rated. It's an irony that Blockbuster, which declines to carry smut, dominates a business that owes its start to porn users.

The VCR removed smut from the neighborhood adults-only porn movie theater and brought it into the privacy of the individual's home. (How all this worked on human sexual compulsion can be seen in the contemporary Hollywood movie *Auto Focus,* director Paul Schrader's take on the sexual obsession of actor Bob Crane, star of 1960s TV.)

Not only the VCR but also portable video cameras and CD-ROMs were all first commercially exploited by producers of X-rated material. To paraphrase *Star Trek,* the id will boldly go where no man has gone before.

It shouldn't be that much of a surprise, then, that sexually explicit content has flooded the Internet. Because of its widespread acceptance, its ubiquity, and its currency, we tend to forget just how recent a development the Internet is. Although its first stirrings came almost fifty years ago, the popular phase of the Internet revolution is really only a decade old.

Like all fresh media technologies, the Internet became a prime medium for sexual expression. Porn providers pioneered such now-staple Internet technologies as streaming video, fee-based subscriptions, pop-up ads, and electronic billing.

What does that mean for the Disturbed Six-in-Tenners, the people who would prefer not to get slapped upside the face with an image of fellatio when they sit down at their computers to check their morning e-mail? What does it mean for parents of children?

In a short ten years, the Internet has become a second technological presence in our lives, behind only television. It represents a shared commons or public square. It is an astonishing realm, perhaps the most democratic, egalitarian, conservative (despite anarchist leanings in the extreme), liberal (despite huge numbers of conservative Web sites), knowledgeable, un-fact-checked, extravagant, dismissive, sex-drenched, mundane, riotous, rule-enforcing, communal, intrinsically personal, truth-telling, lie-spreading, exuberant, petty, untrammeled human sphere ever created.

In other words, like television, the Internet is us. It presents an engrossing portrait of who we are as a society, as a culture, and as human beings as we head into a new millennium.

The Internet also boasts what are quite possibly the nastiest neighborhoods of any town on earth. And its red-light district sprawls crazily.

What kind of sexual content is available online? Let's check into the *Congressional Record,* in 1995, back at the dawn of the popular use of the Internet, to have a U.S. senator describe it for us:

Multimedia erotica; erotica fetish; nude celebrities; pictures black, erotic females; pictures boys; pictures celebrities; pictures children; pictures erotic children; pictures erotica; pictures erotica amateur; pictures erotica amateur females; pictures erotica amateur males; erotica animal; erotica auto; erotica bestiality; erotica bestiality, hamster, duct tape [two of those]; erotica black females; erotica black males; erotica blondes; erotica bondage; erotica breasts. Here is a good one: Erotica cartoons; erotica children; erotica female; erotica female, anal; erotica fetish;

erotica fury; erotica gay men; erotica male; erotica male, anal; erotica Oriental; erotica porn star.

"This goes on and on and on," stated Senator J. James Exon, Democrat of Nebraska, in a Senate speech promoting a bill he had just introduced, the Communications Decency Act. "But it is startling, page after page after page, on screen after screen after screen—free, free of charge, with a click, click, click."

In January 1997 Exon left the Senate, having declined to run for reelection, and the next year his Communications Decency Act was ruled unconstitutional by a unanimous vote of the U.S. Supreme Court.

After me, the deluge. In the decade since Exon stood on the Senate floor and enumerated the almost quaint category listings from an adult bulletin board, sexually explicit content on the Internet has experienced a massive upsurge—a twenty-fold increase in just under a decade. Exon's 1995 catalog was from an adult bulletin board, a fairly obscure Internet ghetto not even connected to the World Wide Web, but the categories he talked about are now amply represented on Web pages just a mouse-click away.

One company that develops Internet filtering software estimated that today there are 260 million adult Web pages out there. As a percentage of the four billion–plus Web pages that a major search engine like Google will link you to, that's a little under 6 percent. In August of 2003, thirty-two million people visited sex-oriented Web sites, a quarter of all people who used the Internet.

For kids, the numbers are more troubling. Forty-five percent of teens say they have friends who regularly view or download smut from the Internet.

You probably don't need statistics to convince you of the ready availability of Internet porn, since you need look no further than the unsolicited e-mail ads in your computer mailbox. But if you doubt it, simply go to your favorite search engine and type in a word. You can choose a word from Senator Exon's list, or think up your own.

(The word "sex," surprisingly, doesn't make a good choice— the initial page of search results yields up a fairly prim collection of health and information sites. "Sex pics," however, returns a bumper crop.)

The search engine I use took less than half a second to produce over 3.5 million Web pages after I typed in a slang word for oral sex.

Senator Exon was never a particular favorite of mine. He employed the kind of over-the-top rhetoric and hysteria-mongering that gives censors a bad name. My libertarian tendencies deny that government intervention, such as Senator Exon was proposing, ever comes to much good. Further, I can see nothing wrong with material from almost every sexual category he lists (with the very important exception of material that sexualizes children) being available to every consenting adult who seeks it out.

The operative words here are "consenting," "adult," and "seeks."

When a nonconsenting adult who is not seeking out smut can be hit with it, or when a ten-year-old child who is led by curiosity can access it, or when an Internet user can blunder into it by mistake, then something is very wrong indeed. Because then it becomes a question of choice, and of privacy—my privacy being invaded for their profit.

If you are connected to the Internet, you have inadvertently encountered smut. Given the sensitivity that many people have to this material, and the deep level of offense it invokes, that is simply unacceptable. It may not offend you, but it may offend your neighbor. And what kind of world do we want to live in, if not one where neighbors look out for each other?

Why does this aggressive assault of sexual images happen? There are reams of material on, say, American colonial history posted on the Web. Why aren't I barraged with spam about Alexander Hamilton? To choose a topic closer to home, why am I not digitally hoodwinked into visiting health Web pages, even though I get plenty of health-oriented spam e-mails?

To understand this, you have to first understand how the business of providing sexually explicit material on the Internet works. The world of Web porn marketing is an aggressive one, a realm of "page-jacking" and "mousetrapping" and other underhanded and illegal sales techniques.

I once sat with my daughter while we both created a Web page on a public Web site called Tripod. Tripod invites any and all Internet users to create Web pages and store them on its site. The company makes a profit by selling advertising that appears on every customer-created page. Free Web pages in exchange for exposure to ads—such is the no-free-lunch dynamic of the Web.

My daughter and I had a fun time creating a fairly silly Web page. For a while, it was all the rage in our house, and then the passion for it faded. But one evening while we were working on it, my daughter mistyped "tripod" into our Internet browser. This misspelling sent us into a sexually explicit spiral, locking us into one X-rated Web page after another.

What had happened, of course, was that unscrupulous Net entrepreneurs had created their own sex Web sites, with addresses that featured common misspellings of popular Internet destinations, including numerous child-oriented sites. So, instead of going to Tripod, we were sent to a hard-core Web site. And once we were there, we became mousetrapped—a situation in which one Web page is programmed automatically to exit into another, related Web page, in an endless, no-exit chain.

In the space of few seconds, my daughter and I experienced a barrage of hard-core images of oral sex, anal sex, bestiality, and S/M. If she had been alone, it would have been a frightening experience for her, as though she had somehow summoned these images by something she had done.

My daughter reports that she and her friends had the same experience when they attempted to locate the Rave Girl clothing store site: they got mousetrapped into an adult site. They had typed "ravegirl.com" instead of "goravegirl.com"—a simple and quite understandable mistake. The metaphorical equivalent to this in the real world would be a huge neon sign advertising the name of a popular youth apparel store. But when gullible customers go through the front doors, the place turns out to be a sex emporium.

There have been repeated anecdotal examples of very young

children getting mousetrapped on an adult site while using a computer at a library, at school, or at home. The problem has been alleviated somewhat since the Federal Trade Commission cracked down in 2003 on Web sites tailored after common misspellings of popular sites (the FTC treated the practice as false advertising).

The FTC also moved against page-jacking, whereby Web pages, including game pages aimed at kids, were copied, along with their embedded commands that allow search engines to locate them. When unsuspecting consumers followed the search-engine link, they would suddenly find themselves viewing a sexually explicit site, often one that was mousetrapped.

Another technique much beloved of Internet sex marketers is the use of deceptive Web addresses to lure the unsuspecting to their sites. The most famous (or infamous) of these is www. whitehouse.com (a sex site), which is not to be confused with www.whitehouse.gov, the official site of the White House. Smut marketers have also at one time or another used variations on NASA's site address, *Reader's Digest,* and Disney.

The end result of this marketing skullduggery—and other practices, such as widely distributed unsolicited e-mail, or spam—is that 20 to 30 percent of Web visitors automatically transferred to adult sites are children. According to Nielsen/ NetRatings, over 15 percent of visitors to adult Web sites are under the age of eighteen.

Why is this happening? The easy answer is that online pornographers have a satanic streak in them, which fiendishly leads them to target children. Judging from the people I know in smut, this characterization gives pornographers way too much credit. Most of them just aren't competent enough to be that Machiavellian. Evil, maybe—that's a judgment call. But evil geniuses? No way.

So why are we assaulted, children and adults both, with unwanted sexually explicit advertisements and material?

Many online services take clear precautions against minors visiting their Web sites. Others do not. The online sex business has become screamingly competitive in the past few years, with operators pouring into the field eager to make a quick buck. Because more companies are pursuing the same finite pool of customers, the whole enterprise is marked by low profit margins. And, like all businesses operating on low margins, the path to profitability lies in high traffic, in getting as many prospective customers as possible to visit your site.

Where smut earns most of its money online is from end-user payments: subscriptions or one-time fees paid to Web sites that provide sexually explicit images and material. Transactions of this sort are made primarily through check or credit card, which acts as a natural age limit that minimizes the exposure of children.

But there is another revenue stream, too, which comes from selling ads that supply customers to other traffic-starved adult Web sites.

Entrepreneurs who provide online sex purveyors with customers are paid by one of three different methods: by the account, by the mouse-click, or by the view. What these companies are doing, when they mousetrap and page-jack and send out spam, is chasing clicks. Again, those who are paid only when a client signs up for an account have no motivation to go after children, since children don't normally have credit cards, the most common form of payment on the Web.

Whether paid by the click or by the view, however, sites make no distinction at all between a child and an adult. A ten-year-old's hand clicking on a Web page has the same value as a thirty-year-old's. A kindergartner viewing a Web site is equal to a retiree. Thus there is no motivation to weed out underage prospects. On the contrary, there is a high motivation not to, since doing so is expensive (cutting into margins even further) and the supplier essentially takes a 20 or 30 percent hit in the number of prospective clients transferred to pay-by-click or pay-by-view adult Web sites.

Pay-by-click or pay-by-view adult Web site ads are the source of the aggressive porn marketing strategies that we and many of our children have experienced online. These practices represent free enterprise stripped of any shred of social responsibility. I don't care what happens to your children, these entrepreneurs seem to say, as long as I get mine.

The use of "teaser" Web pages is one more example of this attitude. While much of the sexually explicit content on the Internet is locked behind subscription-only portals, to be accessed only by use of a credit card, the home or introductory pages for a vast majority of adult Web sites are free to access. This means that there is actually a great deal of material that is either legally obscene or indecent (and certainly obscene for minors) essentially waving free in the Internet breeze.

Three-quarters of adult Web sites feature such explicit home pages. Even without a credit card, a minor may access an incredible variety of sexual imagery. The home pages are essentially billboards that function the way the old carnival sideshow barkers used to, roping in the gullible, shilling for customers. Adult site home pages can be extremely graphic. A twelve-year-old with the right level of curiosity and only a modicum of computer expertise—enough, say, to navigate a search engine—can access images of women with their faces covered with copious amounts of male ejaculate, hard-core oral sex trailers, even graphic teasers for bestiality Web sites.

Mail-order pornography is often advertised for delivery in a "plain brown wrapper." Masking or shielding graphic magazine covers is a fairly common practice in areas of public display. The Internet strips away that plain brown wrapper, and doesn't bother with masks or shields for sexual content. It allows hard-core X-rated content to be advertised—with hard-core samples—in one of the great public commons of our culture.

■ ■ ■

VIRTUAL WORLDS

CHILD PORNOGRAPHY ON THE INTERNET

THE GOOD NEWS IS THAT SEXUAL ABUSE OF CHILDREN BY strangers doesn't occur often. But there's also "bad news": most of those who do abuse children sexually are people with whom a child has an established and trusting relationship. If we let ourselves be guided by statistics, we should be watchful less of strangers than of family members and acquaintances such as teachers, religious figures, or family friends, since they represent over 95 percent of the people who molest our children.

One of the prime worries a lot of parents have regarding Internet safety is the prospect that a child might be lured into an assignation by an online pedophile. The availability of child pornography on the Internet represents concrete evidence that there is a very sick world out there, ready to exploit minors sexually.

But abuse by strangers on the Net is relatively rare. An end-of-the-millennium study indicated that only 3 percent of children had ever been "aggressively" solicited for sex, and that of these, almost half were solicited by other children.

Nevertheless, the sexualization of kids on the Internet disturbs the equilibrium of all those who become upset over seeing children enslaved, battered, raped, and ravaged elsewhere in the world, but who tell themselves "it can't happen here." It can and does happen here, and that the Internet is a medium for making it happen means that a dark cloud hangs over the whole enterprise.

Society should have a zero-tolerance approach to pedophilia, and by and large it does. The one glaring exception is the availability of child pornography on the Internet. Although there have been several high-profile prosecutions of pedophiles who solicit sex online, the production and trade in Internet child pornography has, so far, outstripped the law enforcement effort against it. This is disturbing, because in the very near future, kiddie porn on the Net is going to get a whole lot worse. That's because of certain technological advances, and the way the legal system is set up to deal with them.

In a literal sense, child pornography equals child sexual abuse. The material portrays a crime being committed. For this reason, the courts and legislatures have agreed that such material can be held to a much different legal standard than ordinary images. None of the tests for obscenity need apply. The government efforts are directed against the criminal act of abuse, not the act of expressing or picturing it. Free speech has nothing to do with it.

But what happens when child pornography is produced with no child abuse occurring? Graphic software programs have become so sophisticated that they can create images that are virtually indistinguishable from actual photographs. In other words, pornographers can now make kiddie porn without the participation of kiddies.

I don't know about you, but this strikes me as the kind of dubious march of progress that lists the A-bomb, the car alarm, and call-waiting among its many accomplishments. It also presents a difficult conundrum for the legal system, one it has yet to solve.

On April 16, 2002, the Supreme Court held that a section of 1996's Child Pornography Prevention Act (CPPA) was unconstitutional. The CPPA had expanded the definition of child pornography to include "any visual depiction [that] appears to be a minor engaging in sexually explicit conduct." This clause greatly troubled publishers, writers, producers, and filmmakers, since it seemed to lay them open to liability if they merely recorded instances of sexuality among minors, even if they used of-age actors to do it. A coalition of free-speech advocates challenged the law in court.

"CPPA prohibits speech that records no crime and creates no victims by its production," the Court stated, adding that "the mere tendency of speech to encourage unlawful acts is not a sufficient reason for banning it."

What the ruling did was to place all kiddie porn that is created on computers (without using children) out of reach of child pornography prosecution. Instead, this material is subject to the same obscenity laws that have been on the books for years, during which time we have seen such an enormous explosion of readily available sexually explicit material.

If we rely on current obscenity laws to stop the spread of "virtual" child pornography, the way they have stopped other forms of pornography, then we are in for an onslaught of kiddie porn.

Even though Congress enacted a legislative "patch" in 2003, with the PROTECT Act, its constitutionality remains untested in court, and the law includes a controversial escape clause if the defendant can prove the images were created without the use of a child.

There are other, equally troubling aspects of the Internet in the area of sexual exploitation of children. Commercial production of kiddie porn is minimal. Most of the stuff is privately produced and privately traded. Still, because it is posted on Internet bulletin boards, transferred through servers belonging to Internet service providers, and described in chatrooms, there is a public aspect to it that makes law enforcement's job easier.

Peer-to-peer file sharing (in the parlance of the biz, P2P), in contrast, takes the transaction out of the public realm. It essentially involves two people, each with a computer. File sharing of this type had its highest-profile use in the 1990s, with the controversy over Napster and related music-sharing Web services. But the file being shared need not be an MP3 music file of a hit song. It could be a child porn visual.

That is exactly what is happening in the kid-porn underground. P2P exchanges are proliferating.

The record industry cried well-publicized crocodile tears over this situation. "'P2P' stands for piracy to pornography," said Sony Music honcho Andrew Lack, during a major record industry effort in 2003 to expose kiddie porn on file sharing services.

Given the music industry's habitual sexualization of children, its show of concern was a little hard to stomach (for example, Sony Music puts out Nas, with sample "Big Girl" lyrics, "You're a big girl now, fully grown with your hormones now"). What the push was really about was slowing music piracy. The move against porn merely provided convenient (and bulletproof) political camouflage.

But the record industry's antiporn campaign served to publicize problems with P2P file sharing. Enter three child-oriented names such as "Britney," "Pokémon," and "Olsen twins" into a selected file-sharing service Web site (the General Accounting Office performed a study that actually did this), and half the files will come back as smut. Once again, purveyors of sexual material on the Internet seem intent on piggybacking on kid culture.

Peer-to-peer networks have enormous potential to take information exchange totally out of the public sphere. There are countless legitimate uses for P2P technology. Home computers are so powerful that they can, in effect, act as servers, with no need to store information in any nonprivate venue.

Taking smut out of the public realm is one of the main ideas of this book, but P2P exchange of kiddie porn has troubling ramifications for law enforcement.

Another problematic aspect of the Internet future is the coming boom in real-time services. Once again, commercial sex has been at the vanguard of this technology, whereby live-action material is created specifically for subscribers. Because there is no text or Web page component, real-time sex services are not blocked by most current filtering technology, once the subscriber has joined the service.

A subscriber in New York can receive a streaming real-time video feed from a room in Amsterdam, say, or Hamburg. The subscriber types in commands or suggestions to performers in the room, who in turn perform to specification. In India, children as young as twelve have performed for such operations.

The live-sex component to the Internet is increasingly popular, and its international aspect makes law enforcement difficult if not impossible. Although there have been international agreements against child pornography, variations in what is acceptable in various parts of the world make "obscenity" a relative concept. Mainstream European media has a wide tolerance for nudity that does not transfer to the United States—unless, of course, it is transferred on the Net.

And the Internet is a movable feast. The use of instantaneous forwarding means that a Web site that appears to emanate from Singapore, say, or Switzerland, may actually originate in California or Oregon. Again, this makes law enforcement—and the assumption of social responsibility—problematic.

Often, in terms of confronting child pornography and sexually explicit material, the strengths of the Internet become killing weaknesses. It is a highly decentralized medium, highly mercurial and highly anonymous. There is often no way to determine the veracity, source, or appropriateness of the material we obtain from it.

Widespread use of the Internet has the capability of granting everyone a printing press and making everyone a publisher. That is a superb development in the history of human expression. But it also has its dark side. It allows some people to print child pornography and helps promote them into being publishers and purveyors of the stuff.

■ ■ ■

AD NAUSEAM

PUBLIC SIGNAGE

SUNSET BOULEVARD DIPS BRIEFLY OUT OF THE CITY OF LOS Angeles as it travels west toward the sea, passing through what used to be the jurisdiction of Los Angeles County. The county always had few police and a loose approach to law enforcement, so in the 1920s this stretch of the Boulevard came to be known as Sunset Strip, an area packed tightly with nightclubs, casinos, and brothels. Because of a quirk in the tax laws, many Hollywood agents also located here, contributing to the area's reputation for lax morality.

The nightclubs, at least, are still there, and even after Sunset Strip became incorporated into the town of West Hollywood, it still retained a hint of its former law-skirting flavor. Driving the Strip on a summer afternoon, I wasn't concerned so much with history as with the sex-heavy reality of the present.

The salient feature of today's Sunset Strip is entertainment advertising, a series of massive billboards that turn the thoroughfare into L.A.'s equivalent of Times Square. The billboards of Sunset Strip are huge, extravagant, impossible to miss. You have officially arrived as a Hollywood star when your movie is advertised there—preferably with your sullen airbrushed mug looming large over the bustling clubs and hotels of the Strip.

I've always liked the signs. I like movies, and the over-the-top promotion of them seems in tune with the excitement of the medium. But this trip was different, because the tone of the advertising appeared to have changed. I realized as I drove that the signs were subtly different. The button that the Strip was pushing this time around wasn't "Hollywood" or "cinema."

It was "porn."

The first billboard to catch my eye towered over the Strip's eastern border, a few blocks down from Hollywood High School. Actually, the ad didn't catch my eye so much as reach out and seize my gaze as if it were shooting out sharpened meat hooks. The image was a full-color photo of a pair of unlikely, surgically enhanced female breasts, their nipples hidden by a man's head buried in the cleavage. I didn't quite catch what the sign advertised, so staggered was I by the obviousness of image.

I recognized it immediately. I had seen it countless times before. I even said it out loud: "That's a still from a porn video."

It wasn't, of course, but it might as well have been. There are only so many cards in human sexuality's deck, porn shuffles them endlessly, and this was one of them. I learned later that the sign advertised what is euphemistically called a gentleman's club.

As I continued my drive westward, I realized the porn connection to Sunset Strip advertising was, in quite a few instances, quite literally exact. In a development that I had somehow missed, several of the billboards advertised adult video productions, hard-core, sexually explicit entertainment unavailable at Blockbuster or Wal-Mart or other national chains that decline to carry smut.

"The Vivid Girls," read one billboard, featuring longitudinal shots of a half dozen female porn stars. On the exterior of the Whiskey A-Go-Go, the venerable Sunset Strip club where Jim Morrison and the Doors first grabbed public attention, a sign wrapped around the front of the building: "A billboard isn't the only thing we can erect," cooed the pursed-lipped woman in the double-entendre message, which advertises a line of porn videos.

But the real kicker was a huge sign in the middle of the Strip, afforded pride of place near the famed Chateau Marmont, a locus of decadence in itself (John Belushi died of a heroin-cocaine overdose in one of the hotel's cottages). Depending on your point of view, I was either lucky or unlucky to see it that day, since it was shortly taken down: Vincent Gallo's notorious billboard for his movie *The Brown Bunny*.

The billboard featured a representation of an act of oral sex. The image, a still shot from the movie, was censored—digitally blurred—but still eminently recognizable. "Adults Only," read the ad copy, with an "X-rated" symbol and the needless addendum "In Color." While actress Chloë Sevigny kneels before him, Gallo stands with one hand placed coercively on the back of her head—a familiar porn move known as "skull f**king."

A woman on her knees in front of a man's crotch while he manhandles her. Another card from the porn video deck, only this one was being dealt by an independent movie, distributed to mainstream theaters, in competition at the Cannes International Film Festival (where critic Roger Ebert called it "the worst film in Cannes history").

The Brown Bunny was a one-guy show. Gallo was credited as director, producer, hair stylist, editor, screenwriter, makeup artist, camera operator, production designer, cinematographer, and costumer/wardrober as well as star. After the withering reviews at Cannes, I could imagine that Gallo's distributor, Kinetique, was desperate for publicity. *The Brown Bunny* billboard, featuring pixellated oral sex on Sunset Strip, fit the bill.

Regency Outdoor Advertising, the outfit that put up the billboard, withdrew it after less than a week, but the ad gained worldwide attention and coverage in countless media outlets. Publicity gold. The billboard wound up putting many more dollars in Vincent Gallo's pocket than it cost him. In that sense, it was superbly effective advertising.

As I've tried to be clear about before, I don't believe in censorship. I don't think the government has any business telling me what I can and can't watch in the privacy of my own home. I myself am sick to death of porn, since I have been sorely overexposed to its incredible banality, mind-numbing repetition, and random idiocies. But I nevertheless believe it has its place in our society. We can't deny the fact that sexually explicit entertainment is an incredibly popular multibillion-dollar industry, that people like it, or that adults, both men and women, consume it and voluntarily star in it. Government efforts to control it have been a series of halfhearted blunders.

So, yes, porn has its place. I just don't think that place is looming large over a public street in the heart of the second biggest city in America. The Sunset Strip ads for porn videos and strip clubs and independent movies were all pulled from the same deck. A sexually explicit mishmash has become the common cultural currency.

I was more annoyed than offended. I don't like to be so crudely manipulated, and I don't like the fact that advertisers know they can get to me by presenting certain images. It makes me feel like a puppet on a string. Or some human variation of Pavlov's dog. I enjoy at least the illusion of free will. When I am so crudely denied it, I get angry.

I'm an adult. I didn't have my young daughter in the car that day (although the cars around me were filled with children, all passing by in full view of what was essentially one porn-video still after another). I might be angry, but I wasn't harmed, was I?

I didn't realize right away why I had become so annoyed driving down Sunset Strip that day. But after thinking about it, I understood that the ads, the billboards, the onslaught of sexually explicit material took away a very basic human right, one not fully articulated in the U.S. Constitution, but widely recognized just the same.

The right to be left alone.

I had been assaulted, jerked around, intruded on. My privacy had been invaded by the supposedly private functions of others, splayed out before my eyes.

And I couldn't change the channel.

So, okay. A drive down Sunset Boulevard ruined. No big deal, right? It only affects a minuscule portion of the populace, the thirty or forty thousand people who pass through Sunset Strip every day. Even though Sunset Strip is undeniably public space, it's widely known to be a pretty racy place, so maybe it's just another case of *caveat spector.* Viewer beware. You want to go east-west in L.A.? Take Hollywood Boulevard—well, no, there are billboards all up and down Hollywood, too. Okay, take Olympic, or Wilshire, or Santa Monica. Take a freeway.

But porn billboards aren't limited to a sliced-off section of a single street in Los Angeles. Raunchy signage is popping up all over the country. Our public spaces are becoming increasingly colonized by sexual imagery. My right to be left alone is being challenged everywhere I turn. What is happening on Sunset Strip is only a particularly arresting example of what's happening everywhere.

How about a New York shock jock expressing shock? Elvis Duran, host of Z *Morning Zoo,* the top-rated show on the top-rated radio station in the top-rated New York market, talked about driving into Manhattan on the Long Island Expressway. He found himself confronted by a billboard sign for Larry Flynt's Hustler Club. Two women who "look like they're open for business," as Duran described them, were pictured licking one another's faces.

"I can't help it, I'm offended by this sign," Duran told his morning audience. "I'm trying to fight it, I'm trying not to be an old fuddy-duddy and say 'Put up all the smut you want,' but I was offended by it. Sometimes we are a little too smutty for our own good."

This is from a radio talk-show host who had just finished up a long on-air discussion, with call-ins, about young girls who were getting breast augmentations as high school graduation gifts (Duran and his morning crew primly disapproved of the practice).

Duran's reaction to Flynt's billboard was interesting in that he repeatedly avowed that he liked a "good dirty joke" now and then. He said he wasn't personally offended by the sign, but was "offended for all the kids who were going to see it."

Duran didn't happen to mention it, but Times Square boasted an X-rated billboard that actually targeted kids: a Swatch advertisement for the company's Bunnysutra line. Swatch watches are ragingly popular with children and teens, but Bunnysutra has a watch face that shows copulating rabbits. After gracing Times Square for a period, the Bunnysutra ad, complete with bunnies doing it "doggie-style," was taken down.

Nowhere are the battle lines drawn more clearly over R-rated advertising than in Sin City itself, Las Vegas. In the past few years the sexual content of signs for casinos and strip clubs has been steadily ramped up, until no neighborhood is free from it.

A billboard advertising a rodeo at the Hard Rock Hotel and Casino showed a pair of female legs, panties stripped down to the ankles, with the tagline "Get Ready to Buck All Night." An ad for Lil' Darlin's strip club featured prominent shading on a female model's crotch area. A woman's nipples were clearly displayed on a Pleasures Gentleman's Club billboard. Signs advertising a morning radio program on Las Vegas's Clear Channel–owned KOMP have become raunchy and ubiquitous. "Boobs, Beer and BS," read one.

Ads for Palm Casino invoked one of those recent word coinages that demonstrate a language struggling to keep up with its culture: "neathage," based on cleavage but meaning the exposed bottom part of a woman's breasts, displayed when she wears a skimpy top.

And the explicit ads aren't confined to the Strip—the main entertainment district. Mobile billboards for topless clubs cruise through residential neighborhoods far removed from the casinos. Since 1997, dancers at the Crazy Horse Saloon, "The Crazy Girls," have been advertised on signs affixed to the Las Vegas taxi fleet.

Well, what do expect from a town known as Sin City? If you live in a gambling and entertainment mecca, aren't you at least tacitly agreeing to put up with this kind of stuff? This is, after all, the place Stephen King used to symbolize a modern Sodom and Gomorrah, in his apocalyptic tale *The Stand*. At the end of the world in King's novel, all the evildoers headed to Las Vegas, while all the fine, upstanding folk wound up in Boulder, Colorado.

Seven thousand people move to Las Vegas every month, not all of them evildoers. It turns out that quite a few Vegas residents feel they don't have to choke down whatever the entertainment industry in town pumps out. The city is approaching two million in population now, one of the fastest-growing areas of the country, but it's a somewhat schizophrenic place. The sprawling subdivisions of the north side are far removed from the neon and glitter of the Strip. These are bedrock conservative, heavily Christian areas (the whole state has voted solidly Republican for years).

In other words, Las Vegas is a good microcosm for the push and pull that's going on everywhere in the country, a tug-of-war between the media and entertainment sector on the one hand, and quiet family neighborhoods on the other.

■ ■ ■

THE JEAN POOL

FASHION

JERRY SPRINGER, IN HIS USUAL CALM AND MODERATE STYLE, entitled one of his shows, "My Daughter Dresses Like a Hooker and It's Tearing Our Family Apart." Springer's theatrics aside, I have a gut feeling that the issue of fashion drives much of the disturbance over cultural values that those six out of ten Americans feel.

Part of this, of course, is just the age-old tussle between the generations. Three decades ago, my parents fretted over the length of my hair. But part of it—a large part of it—is the feeling that the way our children dress is a bringing home of a cultural message that most of us are not really comfortable with. How our kids walk out the door on their way to school in the morning (or to a party in the evening) represents the concrete, in-the-flesh, in-your-face result of all the media messages they've been getting all their lives. Fashion is where the pigeons come home to roost.

I recognize a lot of these fashions. In the early 1980s, as a still wet-behind-the-ears midwestern newcomer, I was exposed to the roiling sexual underground in clubs, discos, and parties in the Big City. Although I guess I knew it existed, I had never really encountered the world of adult sadomasochism, red in tooth and claw.

I entered it as an observer, not a participant. I recall actually wanting it to be more bizarre than it was. As a callow bon vivant, I desperately sought to discover a scene that was somehow mysterious, transcendent, passing strange. I didn't find it in the S/M clubs I visited, which thoroughly deflated my expectations. The theatrics I saw there struck me as not worthy of a high school play. The participants were feeble or deluded.

Most of it was loonily pathetic. One place advertised itself as "the friendly S/M club." Another, in Manhattan's now-trendy meat-packing district, was a basement den whose walls were covered with moldy green furze of unknown provenance, like something that would grow on an aging beef carcass.

But one aspect of the scene did strike me as suitably bizarre: the fashions and accoutrements of the most hard-core fetishists. Elaborate confections of metal, leather, or latex (sometimes all three), they were the work of obsessive people with too much time on their hands. Studded dog collars, intricate leather halters, latex hoods. The show itself might be a failure, but the costumes deserved a prize.

Three decades later, many of these rigs are for sale at the local mall.

German fashion photographer Helmut Newton, a.k.a. "Pig Newton" for the demeaning portrayals of women in his work, had a big hand in popularizing S/M and mainstreaming it into advertising. Nowadays David LaChapelle is among the world's top fashion photographers, known as "Little Helmut" for his direct and uncoded use of Newton-style S/M imagery.

In a campaign aimed at getting out the vote, "Declare Yourself 2004," LaChapelle gave us models and movie stars, their mouths cruelly stitched shut with vinyl thread, or ball-gagged with a familiar S/M accoutrement. In a LaChapelle image for a Lavazza ad, the model wears a pink latex hood that is straight out of the clubs. In his ads for the Iceberg clothing line, a model is draped on a couch in Nazi dominatrix regalia, complete with a visored cap labeled "$$"—an oh-so-clever conflation of storm trooper and consumerist imagery.

LaChapelle is only one smutty fashionista among many, and S/M is not the only porn-style imagery prevalent in advertising. In Times Square, a huge billboard embodies what is perhaps the ultimate modern fashion paradox: Kimora Lee Simmons poses for her Baby Phat clothing line completely in the nude but for a pair of sneakers. It's a new oxymoron: naked fashion. I guess the message here might be "The girl needs some clothes."

By an unfortunate chain of events, the stripper has become the default setting for female chic. In a recent issue of *InStyle* magazine, an article described the first jobs of various celebrities. Never mind the witlessness of star worship on parade here, what is interesting is the photo of Mariah Carey that was printed along with the text. The singer stands with a broom in a beauty parlor (her first job). But she is dressed like no hairdresser in the world, in six-inch stilettos, black lace garter belt and panties, and peek-a-boo bra.

What's the relevance of the fashion in this shot? Why is Carey dressed—or undressed—as she is? Does it have anything to do with the subject at hand, which is her first job? No. It's just that if you have a photo of a female in a magazine nowadays, stylists reach for "sex" as a matter of course, as though it were some innocuous tool, like a hairbrush.

More serious is the fact that such overtly sexual fashion advertising extends to publications aimed at teens, especially those targeted to young girls. The clothing brand that has adopted the rubric "fcuk" (which is supposed to stand for "French Connection United Kingdom" but is merely a bad-faith way to drop the f-bomb) placed perfume ads in *Cosmogirl, Teen People,* and other magazines that showed an underwear-clad young couple and the tagline "Scent to Bed." (I've never smelled the perfume, but the ad stinks.)

Bongo jeans ads in *Seventeen* and *Teen People* feature very grown-up images of a model in a see-through fishnet halter, another in a grease-stained baby doll top. An ad for Buffalo jeans that also appeared in teen-targeted publications shows a model with splayed legs and thigh-high boots (with the de rigueur six-inch stiletto heels), her fly unbuttoned to expose her panties, her thumb tugging down the jeans at the crotch.

Fcuk also sells a "too-awful-for-words" T-shirt that reads "Too

Busy to Fcuk." The seventeen-billion-dollar-a-year T-shirt industry aggressively markets to young people, and logos such as
"Bitch" and "Slut" are common. A few of the raunchy T's at least
display a small element of wit, such as the one popular in my
home state of Wisconsin, America's Dairyland: "Smell our dairy
air." Others are just mindless: "Eenie, meenie, minie mo, suck
my d**k you f***ing ho," "I Love Penis," or "I'm on my way
home to masturbate."

The recent catalogs of Abercrombie & Fitch represent master-
works of hebephilia, which is the technical term for sexually
fetishizing teenagers. "Not for sale to anyone under 18," reads the
disclaimer, and the visuals of topless teens inside are indeed
pitched to dirty old men of all ages.

"Sex, as we know, can involve one or two, but what about even
more?" chirps the ad copy in Abercrombie & Fitch's 280-page
"Christmas Field Guide" catalog. "The ménage à trois (three
way) in not an uncommon arrangement. An orgy can involve an
unlimited quantity of potential lovers. Groups can be mixed-
gender or same-sex, friendly or anonymous. A pleasant and su-
persafe alternative is group masturbation."

Wait a minute. I know this stuff. It's porn—porn imagery,
porn logic, porn impure and simple. The boundaries have been
breached between the smut underworld I inhabited back in
the early 1980s and the mainstream world my daughter lives in
today.

That might be what is so upsetting about sex-drenched fashion advertising. TV and the Internet might act as smut-pumps,

but at least the sexual imagery comes in from the outside. It can be controlled, pinched off at its source. But vampy fashion flips the dynamic, making it come from inside the home and head outside. It employs our children to purvey sexually explicit imagery, doing what is literally the fashion industry's dirty work.

■ ■ ■

THE SAVAGE BREAST

POP MUSIC

POPULAR MUSIC IS GRIPPED IN A PERPETUAL RUMBLE WITH forces that judge it too sexual for social good. That may be pop music's function in the cultural universe, to push the boundaries of taste. During jazz's brief heyday as a popular dance music (as opposed to its long reign as a niche passion for aesthetes), it was regularly denounced from pulpits as "the devil's music"—the first in a long line of pop styles to hold that title.

Rock and roll, whose very name is a slang equivalent for sex, has enjoyed an extended reign in the cultural crosshairs. Some of the attacks can be pretty loopy. In Idaho, there is a whole sect, the Church Universal and Triumphant, devoted to the proposition that rap and rock are the work of Satan.

The parents of my generation thought that the music their kids listened to meant that the world was ending. I distinctly recall the feeling of deep adolescent satisfaction I had over my father's reaction to the Beatles' *White Album*. I think it might have been the enclosed full-color glossy of John Lennon, his "freak flag" flying, that sent Dad over the top.

So what is someone to do who loves music, who thinks the attacks on pop are laughably over the top, but who nonetheless believes that perhaps sex-drenched lyrics are not the greatest thing to have pumped into the family household day and night?

What you do, what I have always done, is shut up about it. Lest I be caught on the side of the doomsayers, the album burners, the enemies of a music I love. It is the Bono quandary. Singer Bono of U2 is an icon of cool. I would be loath to do anything to offend my inner Bono. I want to be cool and down with Bono, don't I? How could I not?

We've been through this battle before, in recent memory, and it wasn't pretty. In the early 1980s, back when I was toiling in smut, a then-lowly U.S. senator's wife named Tipper Gore had the temerity to suggest that perhaps the record industry and musicians might want to help the parents of America out. Maybe recording artists could voluntarily place a label on their product that would guide the choices an American family might make about their musical entertainment.

Um, no. Boy, did the musicians of America not want to do that. They reacted to Tipper Gore and the organization she founded, the Parents Music Resource Center, as though they were being attacked by brain-eating zombies.

In a nonpolarized world, a reasonable person could see the worth of a measure that would help sort out the incredible jumble of musical content created in this country.

But this was a polarized world, and these were not reasonable people. The gauntlet was thrown down. Musicians and record-company executives joyously embraced their victim status. They had always read about poor Lenny Bruce, about *Tropic of Cancer* being banned and *Ulysses* having to fight its way into America via the courts.

Now here was their chance to fight the good fight! And they could cast themselves as the champions of free expression! They were in the wrong century to be burned at the stake, but you got the idea that a few were yearning for it.

The music industry wigged out.

"The PMRC's demands are the equivalent of treating dandruff by decapitation," Frank Zappa testified before a U.S. Senate Committee, at the infamous "Porn Rock" hearings in 1985.

Good line, Frank! It doesn't help much to sort out the situation, but it's great rhetoric. In the polarized world of the free-speech debate, then, labeling equals decapitation. Which means you would have to reach pretty far for another metaphor to describe outright censorship—nuclear annihilation of every single carbon-based molecule on the planet, perhaps?

Zappa and singer Jello Biafra of the Dead Kennedys were the high-profile music industry spokespeople, squared off against Tipper Gore and the PMRC. Zappa and Biafra were both ragged-haired neobohemians. Gore was a well-coiffed, experienced advocate of children's rights in other realms, not just this one. Tipper Gore versus Jello Biafra. One was hailed as the courageous champion of the music world, and one became its thoroughly demonized straw dog. I'll let you guess which was which.

So who won? Two decades later, the record industry still

employs the "Tipper Stickers," the voluntary record labeling system for explicit lyrics. Even though at the time Biafra and Zappa described the stickers as the rape of the Bill of Rights, an end to life as we know it, and the death of free expression, pop music has somehow staggered on, healthier (and raunchier) than ever.

Biafra, who was born Eric Boucher in Boulder, Colorado, utilized a good catchphrase. "Don't hate the media," he said. "Become the media." By and large, the media has toed the Jello Biafra line.

Tipper Gore left the PMRC, which sank beneath the waves of history. These days, the Parents Music Resource Center doesn't even have a Web presence, while pop lyricists (as we shall see) still croon away, though they are singing about something other than moon and June.

What was instructive about the fight card of Jello versus Tipper was the total lack of sympathy on the part of the music folks for the position of the other side. The issue was painted in stark terms, black and white, right and wrong, freedom versus censorship. Artists are supposed to be highly empathetic creatures, but no one reached across the divide and said, "Hey, it must be tough raising kids in this kind of environment. I hear what you're saying—maybe we can work together."

There may be hope. In one of those unlikely couplings in which contemporary culture seems to specialize (like Bono and North Carolina's former senator Jesse Helms), the Gore and Zappa families have become close. Though Frank Zappa, who once characterized Tipper Gore as "a cultural terrorist," died in

1993, his wife, Gail, counts the former second lady as a best friend.

But the battle left lasting scars, at least on the delicate sensibilities of defenders of free expression. "Ode to Tipper Gore" is the rock band Warrant's sampler of obscenities recorded live and on tour. Then there is the inevitable "F**k the PMRC" by the ominously named punk group Pistol Grip. Sample lyrics:

F**k the PMRC
Decisions to be made by almighty Tipper Gore
But I don't want to leave it to a crazy Christian whore

Compare the thoughtfulness of Tipper Gore's warning-label campaign (she was always very careful to say she was against censorship) with the ranting hyperbole of these lyrics.

The PMRC may be no longer, but it is immortalized not only in lyrics but also through Internet ghost stories designed to frighten children and musicians.

"This month marks the anniversary of a dark and grim moment in the history of the United States," intones one such Web memorial, with prose that deserves the purple heart, "where self-proclaimed guardians of morality drove the cold, sharp knife of censorship deep into the heart of free speech."

Freedom-Man fighting the forces of prudery! It's such a high, fine role that it must be hard to let go. Another Web site—twenty years after the fact!—allows visitors to knock the teeth out of a portrait of Tipper Gore, blacken her eye, and bloody her mouth.

So, literally and figuratively, Tipper has been beaten and the PMRC vanquished, chased from the field. And free speech, despite the cold, sharp knife in its heart, lives on.

Did the effort back then have any substantial effect on the content of music today? Let's sample the Top 10 songs from a random week in summer 2004. The bestselling, most-played singles for the week: "Lean Back," "Sunshine," "Goodies," "Slow Motion," "Turn Me On," "Dip It Low," "My Place," "Confessions Part II," "Pieces of Me," and "Move Ya Body."

Detect a theme? Sex is on the minds of the boys and girls of the Top 10, sex and only sex, and a particular kind of sex, too. Yes, some of the songs come in explicit versions, but it goes beyond that. Way beyond. The majority of these songs are miniature sex manuals, specifying the techniques required.

> Said my niggas don't dance
> We just pull up the pants and do the rock-away
> Now lean back, lean back, lean back, lean back
> —"Lean Back"

> Just answer your phone whenever I call
> Cause I'm riding on chrome whenever I ball
> I like them short and tall but not too thick
> I just walk in the spot and take my pick
> And they wanna roll cause they like my style
> And when I pop my collar I make them smile
> I need a lady in the streets but a freak in the sheets
> —"Sunshine"

I got a sick reputation for handlin' broads
All I need me is a few seconds or more . . .
Throw all the dirt you want it's no use.
You still won't have a pinup in a fabulous room
On her back pickin' out baskets of fruit
—"Goodies"

I'm a d**k thrower, her neck and her back hurting
Cutthroat will have her like a brand new virgin
—"Slow Motion"

One hand on the ground
And bumper c**k sky high
Whining hard on me
Got the Python
Hollerin' for mercy
—"Turn Me On"

Dip it low
Pick it up slow
Roll it all around
Poke it out like your back broke
Pop pop pop that thing
I'ma show you how to make your man say "Ooo"
—"Dip It Low"

We never had a problem gettin' it done
Disagreed upon a lot, but the sex wasn't one

And check it, I know you get excited
When I come round and bite it
  —"My Place"

From head to toe I feel your flow
Thighs get stronger (stronger)
Party seems longer (Longer)
Make me really want ya
Don't stop movin', you're making me hot
  —"Move Ya Body"

Of the two Top 10 songs not quoted above, Usher's "Confessions Part II" is a sexual morality tale, about a guy working up the courage to tell "the woman I love" that "a woman I hardly know" is going to have his child. That leaves Ashlee Simpson, Jessica's little sister, to give us a nonexplicit, generic love song, "Pieces of Me." It's the only entry in the Top 10 that—surprise!—doesn't specifically reference sex.

Nine out of ten. There is only one subject in the whole chart-topping world, and that's sex. How to do it, how I did it, how you should do it, how we are going to do it.

I am so glad the efforts a few decades back of the terrible censors in the Parents Music Resource Center didn't succeed in curtailing the wonderful creativity of our recording artists. That would have been a tragedy beyond measure. These lyricists might actually have had to dream up songs about another subject besides sex.

Far from being all too human, I catch a whiff of the robotic in these lyrics. Must have sex now. The reverse puritanism beggars description. It's as though these songwriters were all communally lobotomized, their brains purged of everything except a single primal urge. They resemble Chauncey Gardiner, the imbecilic hero played by Peter Sellers in the movie *Being There*.

"I like to watch," Chauncey repeats over and over, and everyone takes it for genius. "I like sex," repeat these Top 10 songwriters.

Yes, yes, and I like my cigar. But I take it out of my mouth every once in a while.

■ ■ ■

SILENT THRILL

VIDEO GAMES

AT AN UPSCALE PRIVATE SCHOOL IN A SUBURBAN TOWN NEAR where I live, an English teacher and adviser to the senior class expressed his shock at his students' first choice for a prom theme: "Pimps and Hos."

"They were serious," the teacher said, laughing in disbelief. "They had the decorations designed, and instead of a promenade they were going to do a 'perp walk.'"

A California-based company called Brands On Sale sells tyke-sized pimp and ho costumes for Halloween. The pimp suit is one of the company's biggest sellers, and they can outfit the whole family, parents, children, and dog. In development: a pimp outfit for infants. Other costumers sell "Pimp Daddy" or "Mac Daddy" outfits, blue velvet with faux leopard trim.

Welcome to the brothel. "Pimp" and "ho" have now become all-purpose terms of address for many teenagers, invoked, no doubt, with proper adolescent irony, but enjoying great currency nonetheless. MTV boasts an autocustomizing program called Pimp My Ride, while the rap artist Nelly shills a drink called Pimp Juice.

We can thank a computer games company called Rockstar for adding immeasurably to the popularity of such icons from the world of prostitution, since it produces a bestselling video game called Grand Theft Auto: Vice City. GTA, as it is known among cognoscenti, is a simulated crime game in which the players are pimps, having sex with and then murdering their hooker victims as they rampage through the mean streets of an urban landscape (extra points for hit-and-run killing of pedestrians).

Rockstar will eventually rake in an estimated four hundred million dollars on GTA, a healthy slice of a video games industry that grosses almost seven billion dollars in the United States and almost twenty billion dollars worldwide. Grand Theft Auto has achieved the kind of market penetration that most products never approach, to the point where it has heavily influenced youth culture. It's a pimps and ho's world, and this video game helped make it that way.

"I'm for freedom of speech but Grand Theft Auto is heinous," said *Washington Post* columnist Mike Wilbon. "The people who put it together should be stoned in the street." Street stoning would probably earn Wilbon a few points if he were playing GTA, but his is merely a small sample of the wrath directed at Rockstar.

But it's all okay, right? GTA: Vice City and its sequels, GTA3 and GTA: San Andreas, are both rated M for "mature" by the Entertainment Software Rating Board, the industry's self-regulatory body. So there is no possible way that minors are getting access to GTA, right?

Think again. Seventy percent of teenage males under the age of seventeen report they have played GTA. In December 2001, the Federal Trade Commission released a study that showed 78 percent of children between the ages of thirteen and sixteen were able to purchase M-rated games. The FTC also found that video game companies were deliberately marketing M-rated games to minors, just as the tobacco cartels had targeted children previously.

That all presents a picture of a video games ratings system that is full of holes, and a technology that is easily transferred, borrowed, or illegally acquired. It's enough to further disturb a Disturbed Six-in-Tenner.

GTA isn't the only sex-heavy game out there. BMX XXX is a smutty take on off-the-road bike racing, complete with topless female riders with options for choice of breast size. Pimps and ho's again figure in heavily, with players able to pick up a hooker and transport her to another locale in the game. Dead or Alive: Xtreme Beach Volleyball features what has become standard issue for video games: top-heavy bikini-clad female avatars.

The tide of sexually explicit games hasn't crested yet. In what has to be the most pathetic vicarious thrill on the market, Playboy: The Mansion allows players to direct nude photo shoots, host parties, and suck up to celebrities, all while wearing the pajamas of Hugh Hefner. The players choose attributes of the female models, including the color of their panties and their breast size (choose from big breasts, bigger breasts, and biggest breasts).

Playboy magazine itself broke ground when it published a photo spread of computer-generated images, female video game avatars who "posed" nude for the magazine. Popular characters from Mortal Kombat and the Tekken series, as well as such female avatars as Red Ninja and Bloodrayne, helped blur the line between physical and virtual sex.

But *Playboy* represents the tamer end of the sexual spectrum in video game raunch. Singles, a Sims-like game, and Leisure Suit Larry, a reprise of an early explicitly sexual video game, push the boundary of M (for mature) and AO (for adults only) ratings.

While video console sales (for such devices as Xbox and PlayStation) are dominated by action, racing, sports, and first-person shooter games tailored to the teenage male, computer-based games sell more strategy, children's, and simulation games. But the recent skew toward more explicit sex has hit both computer and video games.

Most of the research done regarding the impact of video games has been on violence. In an unprecedented unanimous condemnation, the country's most respected public health groups lined up in 2001 to say that viewing entertainment violence increases aggressive attitudes and behaviors, particularly in children. The groups are a who's who of the public health establishment, including the American Medical Association, the American Academy of Pediatrics, the American Academy of Family Physicians, and the American Academy of Child and Adolescent Psychiatry.

GTA features a toxic mix of sex and violence, vending two assaults for the price of one. Computer and video gaming reaches an astonishing percentage of America's children, boasting almost television-like numbers: over 95 percent of kids ages two to seventeen have played a video game. With games such as GTA making sport out of rape, video game producers resemble sociopaths we've collectively hired to babysit.

Maybe stoning in the street is too good for them.

■ ■ ■

DROPPING DIME

PHONE SEX

EVERY HOUSEHOLD APPLIANCE THAT CAN POSSIBLY SERVE AS A conduit for sex has been put to work: the computer, the video game console, the stereo, the TV, and the telephone. Coming soon, no doubt, are X-rated toaster ovens and adult steam irons.

But the telephone got there first.

Phone sex is a $1 billion market in this country, $4.4 billion worldwide. I was there in the early days. At the beginning of the 1980s an editor named Jeffrey Goodman worked in an adult universe parallel to mine, heading up such porn glossies as *Oui*, *High Society*, and *Cheri*. Goodman's amorality was the stuff of legend even in the determinedly immoral world of New York smut. We used to laugh at his antics, his grasping after the thinnest dime, his willingness to exploit for gain any human who crossed his path.

Goodman was among the first porn editors to discover the incredible amount of money to be made off phone sex. When advances in telephone technology made it possible to cash in on the volume of calls to a particular 900 number, he crowed about the opportunity this presented to would-be smut moguls.

"One 900 number, two hundred thousand dollars a month," he said. "Five 900 numbers, one million dollars a month. And the best thing about is that the phone company does your billing and sends you the payment every month. I get checks from AT&T!"

Goodman loved that. A huge Wall Street corporation, listed on the stock exchange, a bulwark of American capitalism, sending him checks for his smut business.

"You want to know why pay phones in New York still cost only a dime?" he asked. "All over the country, they cost a quarter now, but not in New York. That's because the public utility commission won't let them raise pay phone rates, because the phone company is raking in such big profits on phone sex lines."

Goodman sank out of sight eventually, probably retiring with his phone sex millions, but I always kept an eye on the New York pay phones after that, and they did indeed cost only a dime for much of the 1980s. While I didn't trust Goodman's reasoning (or anything else about him), it made an ironic sort of sense.

"Dropping dime" was street slang for ratting someone out, calling the police from a pay phone. "Dropping quarter" didn't have the same ring to it. The telephone company's profit participation in the burgeoning number of sex services made it all happen.

Phone sex holds a minor place in the constellation of sexual material to which minors can be exposed. Many phone-sex services require a credit card for use, thus precluding a child's inadvertent or unauthorized access. And the phone company offers blocking services for direct-dial 900 lines.

But keeping in mind that single thin dime it took to use a pay phone in New York throughout the 1980s, we might want to ask what other large American corporations have benefited from having one hand in the porn till.

It turns out there are quite a few. When you have a multibillion-dollar business as active and sprawling as the business of smut, there is bound to be overlap, interplay, trafficking of one kind or another. But it is more than that. Porn is intricately threaded into the fabric of American commerce. Everything we do is stitched with it.

The nation's biggest cable company, Comcast, grosses fifty million dollars annually from adult programming—an amount that has increased every year for the last decade. Every major cable company distributes at least some graphic sexual content to its subscribers, much of it hard-core porn. One industry analyst estimated that satellite services such as DirectTV and EchoStar gross "a couple hundred million, maybe as much as $500 million, off of adult entertainment."

Half of the guests in such big hotel franchises like Holiday Inn or Marriott purchase smut movies on in-room pay-per-view systems. This represents almost pure profit for the chains. According to some estimates, smut represents 70 percent of in-room profits. Six-dollar beers from the minibar have got nothing on twenty-dollar porn films on pay-per-view.

Far be it from me to advocate limits on good old-fashioned American free enterprise. But corporate collusion in the world of smut has to be factored in when we raise our voices to demand that boundaries be imposed on the sexually explicit material flooding every corner of our lives. It's frustrating to see corporate America mouth platitudes about good citizenship, yet at the same time be all too willing to sell our children down the line in the interest of profit.

Frustrating, but perfectly human. Less explicable is the stance of the firebrands of the left, who constantly rail against the excesses of American capitalism. Somehow, though, one very bloated enterprise with ten billion dollars in estimated annual revenue gets a free pass. You'll never see a World Trade Organization–style demonstration against smut.

Which recalls the fact that in Stalinist Russia, a choice had to be made about which technology the state apparatus would invest in: the telephone or the loudspeaker? Both were coming into wide use at about the same time, but the threadbare Soviet economy could only afford to develop one. Tellingly, Stalin chose the loudspeaker. He favored the one-voice-speaking-to-many model over the much harder to control many-voices-speaking-to-many.

The constant dunning of the human libido in American culture sometimes reminds me of the propaganda broadcasts of totalitarian regimes, a droning repetitive drilling into the brain. It comes to us via the telephone, the TV, the Internet. We might have many voices. But too often it seems we only have one message.

■ ■ ■

THE RETURN OF PORN CHIC

BOOKS

FOR A BRIEF, ADDLED MOMENT IN THE EARLY 1970S, A hard-core porn film represented a perfectly okay choice for a date movie, a swinger's club called Plato's Retreat attracted hordes of middle-class enthusiasts, and pornographers were interviewed on talk shows and in magazines as though they were important revolutionaries. The last vestiges of 1950s morality were being sloughed off, and people—especially men ("The sexual revolution was for men," said ringside witness Yoko Ono)— basically lost their minds.

Porn films as date movies always recall Travis Bickle, the seriously psychotic Robert DeNiro character in *Taxi Driver*—a film classic made at the tail end of the porn chic era. When Travis finally takes out his dream girl Betsy (played by Cybill Shepherd), he brings her to a Times Square smut film on their first evening together. The look of distress that passes over Betsy's face isn't so much triggered by what's up on the screen (she can barely look at the pseudo-anthropological smut that's being presented). Her reaction measures the uncrossable gulf between her and her erstwhile date. Another romance gone down in flames.

Deep Throat, the 1972 date movie of the year, was made for twenty-five thousand dollars by a Queens hairdresser named Gerard Damiano. It is said to have grossed over six hundred million dollars worldwide, a number no doubt wildly inflated, but at even a quarter of that box office, it is among the most successful independent films of all time (eat your heart out, Michael Moore). Damiano, a gravel-voiced former celebrity when I met him, never saw a dime of the money. "The mob got it all," he said simply.

A decade after porno chic, in 1981, when Goldstein introduced me to Damiano, Plato's Retreat's Larry Levenson, and other luminaries in the murky firmament of smut, the business had outlasted its fifteen minutes of fame. There was nothing chic about it any longer.

Damiano was a solid enough guy, but he never quite left behind the flavor of his home borough. Levenson, the self-appointed spokesperson for wife-swapping and the swingers' movement, was spectacularly thick-witted. He went to jail for tax fraud because he kept two sets of books for his nightclub, one cooked, one raw. Which plenty of people do, but Levenson got mixed up and gave tax auditors the wrong set. Meeting him, hanging out with him, visiting him in prison, I was consistently amazed that someone so stupid could even remember to breathe.

In early 1980s, the distribution for *Screw* and a lot of other porn mags was controlled by a business that was in turn controlled by the Gambino mob family. Goldstein got regular visits by the capo whose thumb he was under: Robert "DB" DiBernardo, another mook straight out of central casting. I recall being ushered into Al Goldstein's office to meet DB as though to an audience with the Pope. He was treated with hushed awe as he stirred his espresso with a tiny spoon. Later, much later, DB was murdered on the orders, investigators say, of Gambino boss John Gotti, disappearing from a beach in Florida, his body never found.

Goldstein, Damiano, Levenson, DiBernardo. Ah, yes, porn chic. Yet more evidence that when the subject is sex, normally capable human beings rush to divest themselves entirely of their reason.

Now, three decades later, porn chic is back. In the past few years or so, under the onslaught of sexually explicit material on the Web, the bombardment of sexual innuendo on TV, the eroticized twist of fashion and advertising, we have arrived, once again, where the business of sex is fashionable, glamorous, high-profile.

The porn chic whirlwind has hit hardest in an odd venue, the local bookstore. Odd because book publishing is traditionally the stodgiest of the media businesses, the most intellectual, the least sexy. Compared to computer gaming and the Internet, it has an especially tenuous hold on the younger audience. Quite a few young people agree with Jimmy Durante's old laugh line "I read a book once. I didn't like it."

Porn, ever popular with postadolescent males, might be a way for book publishers to lure the younger crowd back in.

Paging through a wave of smut-themed books, I can only cite a book reviewer's memorable sentiment about the French poet Chapelain: "A new horror has been added to accomplishment of reading."

The mega-smash bestseller *How to Make Love Like a Porn Star: A Cautionary Tale* came to us with impeccable credentials. It was published by Judith Regan of ReganBooks, among the savviest editors of our time (she'd argue, not without reason, that she *is* the savviest). Regan cut her teeth on pop culture during her days working at the *National Enquirer* and has an unerring sense of what appeals to large sectors of the public. *Porn Star* was written by Jenna Jameson, with Neil Strauss, formerly a music critic for the *New York Times* who was fired from the newspaper as a result of his participation in the project.

"I don't publish pornography," sniffed Regan to the *Times*.

Pornography, of course, is in the eye of the beholder. Let's dip into *Porn Star,* shall we?

"The women in 'Playboy' seemed so much more mature," explains porn-star-turned-author Jenna Jameson about her early aspirations. "So I set my sights on a more appropriate goal: a magazine my father used to have around the house, like 'Penthouse' or 'Hustler.'"

Or, another through-the-looking-glass statement from Jenna and Neil: "A girl really has to have her head and life together to do porn."

This all brings to mind another oxymoron: bottomlessly shallow. *Porn Star* contains graphic descriptions of sexual techniques, an attempt, I fear, to fulfill the oh-so-alluring promise of the title. But the real substance of the book details the ghastly time that a girl named Jenna Massoli had of it while growing up in Las Vegas. Rape victim, stripper, porn star. Connect the dots.

Reading the book has the same feel as moving into a trailer park. The relentless low pitch of the prose, in fact, turns the whole world into one big trailer park, and there is no way out.

Judith Regan published Howard Stern's bestseller *Private Parts,* and Jenna squeals for a whole chapter about landing a part in the movie version of Stern's book. Her part is "Mandy," the first girl to appear nude on Howard's radio show (nudity on radio being one of Stern's pioneering stunts). At the film's opening she meets a rock star and the two begin to date. That's what passes for a happy ending nowadays.

Porn Star is a book that very clearly wants it both ways. It wants to strut *and* moralize. There's the subtitle, *A Cautionary Tale,* which hints at Hayes Code–style punishment for sins. As a sometime ghostwriter myself, I appreciated Neil Strauss's heavy lifting, trying to gussy up the material as best he could. Each section of the book leads off with a quote from Shakespeare's sonnets.

"You can't shine smutch," my German grandmother used to say, using an idiomatic word related to the title of this book. She meant that you can work hard at making something shine, you can dress it up and put Shakespeare in its mouth, but if it's smutch, in the end it will stay smutch.

After reading Jenna Jameson's tome, all 579 pages of it, there is really only one human (and humane) reaction: I don't *want* to make love like a porn star. The color and black-and-white photographs with which the book bulges show a slight, pretty young woman, someone who to my eyes is about as sexy as a wheel chock. The anti-Marilyn.

There's no disputing taste, of course, and legions of folks think Jenna Jameson is the tartiest tart around. "Awww, hunny, yer so boo'ful," we would have said back at *Screw,* mocking the throaty, lust-choked mutterings of the raincoat crowd.

No doubt those legions of Jenna fans will line up for the other offerings at the local bookstore, like *How to Have a XXX Sex Life,* by the same Vivid Girls I saw vamping on a Sunset Boulevard billboard. Again, no thanks. You want to tell me how to have joyless, mechanical, existentially parched sex? Sorry, I know you ladies might find it hard to believe, but I don't *want* to have an XXX sex life.

But in case you do, there's plenty of advice available down at Ye Olde Corner Bookstore, including titles for those who desire an existence just as ghastly as Jenna Jameson's: *How to Become a Porn Director: Making Amateur Adult Films, 1-2-3 Be a Porn Star! A Step-By-Step Guide to the Adult Sex Industry,* or *The Pimp Game: Instructional Guide.*

"Porn lit," they are calling the genre.

"Sex without love is an empty experience," says Woody Allen, "but as empty experiences go, it's one of the best." All right, it's a joke, I know, and it would be boorish to take it as anything but a laugh line. But I disagree. I'd prefer a lot of other empty experiences to the ones offered up in *Porn Star.*

"Sex is dirty if it's done right." Another Woody Allen laugh line, but it embodies a human truth that might be best kept locked away deep in the back cabinet of the psyche, not paraded out full force in our bookstores.

I recall there were quite a few artists and writers who wanted to traipse through the *Screw* offices in the early 1980s. They came because they were looking for material, or because they were curious. John and Yoko gave an interview, and *Dr. Strangelove* screenwriter Terry Southern occasionally wrote for the rag. *Hollywood Confidential* author James Ellroy (the best crime writer of our age) spent a few days back then poking around the offices.

Just as crows are attracted to bright objects, writers and journalists are sometimes attracted to the dark. It's their inversion of porn chic. These folks would be dismayed to see Jenna Jameson's book breaking sales records. Too much light ruins their fantasy. How louche can this stuff be, if it's on the bestseller lists?

In the winter of 1982 the *Screw* offices got another author visit, from novelist Philip Roth (the absolute best writer of our age). Roth spent a few hours with Goldstein, then came upstairs to speak with the boys in editorial. My fellow editors Josh Friedman, Manny Neuhaus, and I were thrilled. We stumbled all over each other trying to impress the visitor.

I trotted out a few of my ghostwritten Goldstein editorials for the great man to peruse. Roth scanned them for a moment and then posed a cutting question: "But who reads it?"

I was momentarily flustered. "It's art for art's sake," I said, and Roth laughed.

But that's the sad truth behind porn chic. For all its time in the center ring of today's media circus, nobody cares. Writers and artists work overtime, in magazines, books, movies, and music, pumping up human sexuality into something romantic, mysterious, transcendent. But it remains what it is. You can't shine smutch.

"Sex should be like drinking a glass of water" runs Vladimir Lenin's famous apothegm, although it turns out the Russian revolutionist didn't even come up with the line himself, but stole it from one of his mistresses. She meant that sex should be banal, demystified, everyday. It's part of human biology. Efforts to make it anything more finally come off as silly or, in Jenna Jameson's case, mawkish.

A short year after he showed up at *Screw*'s offices, Philip Roth turned his research there into a tour-de-force portrait of a pornographer in his novel *The Anatomy Lesson*. He spent at most four hours at *Screw* that afternoon, but he absolutely nailed Goldstein to the wall in his fictional portrayal, as incisive and penetrating a dissection of another human being as any I have ever read.

The pelt is still on display for anyone who cares to pick up the Roth novel. I was there, I had seen Roth ask questions, poke around, converse. But when I read the results, I was awestruck. I had known Goldstein for a year. Roth spent a few hours with the man. How could anyone penetrate that deeply in that short of time? But Roth managed to, and I guess that's what genius is.

Because I experienced it from the inside, I know that porn chic is a lie. Roth discovered this, or knew it intuitively after a brief visit. I've been in that world, and I know just how un-chic porn really is.

In the past few decades, the courts have pretty much decided that books can no longer be declared legally obscene. Nothing text-based is prosecuted anymore, only visuals. So porn lit gets a free pass. But there are standards other than legal ones, or there should be. One standard is that nobody will be much helped by stories that present life as one long grim slide into the sty.

The title of *How to Make Love Like a Porn Star* represents false advertising. I guess you can't call a book *How to Behave Like a Crank-Addled Moron,* but that's what Jenna Jameson delivers. If you want to know what it really means to make love like a porn star, you might want to try the greats, such as Ibsen, Roth, *Moll Flanders,* or even John O'Hara's *BUtterfield 8.* The real story is out there, but you won't find in the pumped-up pages of porn lit.

CHAPTER NINETEEN

■ ■ ■

MAXIMIZATION

MAGAZINES

ARE ALL PUBLISHERS MAD? IS THAT A NECESSARY ATTRIBUTE TO get into the publishers' club, that you be larger than life, out of control, nuttier than thou? It certainly seems that way. At least, all the magazine publishers I've ever met have thought themselves alpha visionaries, which in the real world translates into their being bombastic bullies. That may be what it takes to survive in the Darwinian world of periodical publishing.

You can't argue with the success of Felix Dennis, who publishes *Maxim, Stuff, Blender, The Week,* and other magazines. Dennis came up during the 1970s underground press movement in Britain, with the pioneering alternative newspaper *Oz.* He is no stranger to the indecency debate, being one of the three defendants in the United Kingdom's infamous *Oz* obscenity trial in 1971. But it was publishing computer magazines and ownership of a computer mail-order business that made him richer than God—or at least the sixty-fifth richest individual in Britain.

Maxim began 1995 as Felix Dennis's entry into the already crowded field of "lad" magazines in the United Kingdom, publications such as *Loaded* and *FHM* (originally abbreviating, stupidly enough, "for him magazine"). Lad mags catered to the beer-and-skittles crowd, the soccer louts, the still-single twentysomethings who lived with their mums.

In the United Kingdom, *Maxim* tanked. Or at least it lagged in the back of the lad pack, not particularly popular, certainly not a profit-making standout in Dennis's stable of publications. Then, in April 1997, he brought *Maxim* to the United States.

It was a smash hit.

In less than five years, *Maxim* far outstripped the circulation of such old-guard standards as *Esquire* and *GQ* to become the bestselling "men's lifestyle" magazine in America. Not content with *Maxim*'s 2.5 million monthly circulation, Dennis launched a "sister" magazine, *Stuff,* that was soon selling over a million copies every month. Taken together, the *Maxim/Stuff* combine outsells every other male-oriented magazine in the annals of American publishing, including *Playboy* and *Penthouse.*

"We don't use the 'P-words' around here," Dennis always mock-hushed any discussion of *Playboy* and *Penthouse* around the Maxim offices. For good reason. He didn't want his flagship magazine tarred with the smut brush.

But that's only avoiding the obvious: *Maxim* is, of course, a just-this-side-of-soft-core alternative to smut mags, skirting the boundary between PG-13 and R. This was the secret to *Maxim*'s success—it was a version of *Playboy* that young male readers could, without too much embarrassment, peruse in public, read on the airplane, leave on the coffee table. There is a lot of cheese-cake in *Maxim*, with three major pictorials of nearly nude mod-els, actresses, or minor celebrities in every issue, plus random collateral bikini photos larded into features and service articles.

One aspect of *Maxim*'s success was its similarity to another publishing phenomenon, this one targeted to women: the chron-ically sex-addled *Cosmopolitan*. Both magazines featured copious amounts of advice aimed at alleviating the cluelessness of the reader regarding sex, fashion, sex, work, sex, consumerism, and did I mention sex? But since male egos were frightened of ap-pearing as clueless as they really were, *Maxim* was forced to couch its advice columns in flip humor and smarmy attitude.

By the time I was hired on (briefly, for two issues) as a con-sulting editor, *Maxim* had taken over the universe. I guess it only seemed that way, gazing at the publications displayed at the cor-ner newsstand. Every magazine aimed at males slavishly copied the *Maxim* formula of running a half-dressed female on its cover. *GQ? Esquire? Details?* They all came to resemble *Maxim*.

In retrospect, it all seemed screamingly obvious. How to at-tract young men to a magazine? Print a scantily clad woman on the cover. Who knew?

But combined with the display policies of women's magazines, many of which had long ago adopted the practice of using cover shots of half-dressed females, suddenly it seemed that the whole world had gotten *Maxim*ized.

The bald manipulation that lies behind these magazine cover shots offends me. Publishers know they can get to me. Just an-other jerk on the chain.

Magazines such as *Maxim* and *Cosmopolitan* have healthy subscription bases, but they live and die by newsstand sales. In *Maxim*'s case, to hit the circulation rates it guarantees its advertisers, the magazine must sell an astonishing million copies every month off the newsstand. This means display strategy is crucial. That's the reason for the raunchy covers on *Maxim, Cosmo,* and so many other magazines. Success depends on a quick-trigger response to the cover. And what could be more quick trigger than sex?

But if raunchy covers yield higher sales, doesn't that mean the public endorses smut? I've heard this argument all my life, but it's bogus. Profitability does not equal popularity. What about all those people who don't buy *Cosmo?* What about all those people who believe its tasteless coverlines might not be the best reading material for children? Out of 250 million people in America, one million or so might purchase *Cosmo* every month. That's not exactly a ringing endorsement of the sex-heavy display policies of magazine publishers.

I never had anything to do with the cheesecake end of *Maxim,* which seemed to happen at photo shoots far away from the cluttered Midtown Manhattan offices of the magazine. But I became a regular contributor of another element of the *Maxim* formula, what Felix Dennis labeled "the gritty read." These were crime or disaster articles that resembled the "true adventure" stories in 1950s men's magazines such as *True West, American Manhood,* or *Stag.*

I recognized the atmosphere of the *Maxim* offices from the period that I worked in smut. The staff was overwhelmingly young and male. The humor was raunchy, rude, and feckless. For all of

Felix Dennis's announced intent of erecting a firewall between his magazines and the world of porn, not a few of the staffers were, like myself, graduates of that world.

The influence ran the other way, too. One of my editors at *Maxim*, Jim Kaminsky, was hired on as editorial director of *Playboy* for a while. A lot of mainstream mags were poaching lad-mag talent: *Rolling Stone* hired an *FHM* editor, and Mark Golin, another *Maxim* editor, was hired away to head up *Details*.

"You guys think you can get away with anything," groused a female staffer once, after we had concocted a particularly vile *Maxim* article on I forget what (though it probably had something to do with sex). I recall that the core group of male editors merely grinned and nodded back at her. Get away with anything? That sounded good to us.

It's wrong to criticize *Maxim* for its frat-boy humor, abbreviated attention span, and formulaic presentation. "It is what it is" was the faint encomium I always used in defending the magazine to its detractors. There is no doubt a place for *Maxim* in the American publishing universe.

What is distressing is that it sometimes seems that *Maxim*'s place is the only place, that other publications are crowding toward it like moths to a flame. Yes, imitation is the sincerest form of flattery, but when out of forty magazines displayed in the newsstand, thirty-nine have women in bikinis on the cover, something has gone seriously awry with the proverbial spice of life.

Once again, as it had with television and the Internet, sexual content overpowered a niche of American media, the magazine.

Once again, it was difficult to "change the channel." When all magazines resemble one another, choice becomes irrelevant. And, since magazine covers are often prominently displayed in public, they impose on the sensibilities of those who might be offended by them, in ways that other media do not.

Say you are adamant about limiting the intrusion of other people's sexual content into the privacy of your world. You could conceivably "blow up your TV," as John Prine used to sing. And you could refuse to go online. But magazine covers displayed in public are different. Along with billboard advertising and fashion, they are "nondisengageable." We see them whether we want to or not, inadvertently or unintentionally, as do our children.

Felix Dennis and the gents up at *Maxim* want to rub your faces in it (I know this to be true, because I've been one of them). So do all the other magazine publishers and editors who know that a sexy cover shot is the equivalent of squeezing a surefire human trigger. Thus at the grocery store, on newsstands, and in airports, we are gifted with blitzkrieg images of sexual excess. And we the erstwhile targets of this assault have stood by and accepted it as just another aspect of the *Maxim*ized modern world.

■ ■ ■

A CASE OF THE CREEPS

MOVIES

COMING SOON TO A MULTIPLEX NEAR YOU, THE NONPORN PORN film. John Cameron Mitchell is an obscure director of independent films, his single claim to fame being *Hedwig and the Angry Inch,* about a drag queen rock star. Mitchell has announced his next project will be *Shortbus,* an explicit hard-core art film. He's having trouble raising money for it.

If *Shortbus* gets made, it will join Vincent Gallo's *Brown Bunny* in the race for independent film to emulate porn. Mitchell promises there will be actual hard-core sex shown onscreen. But he hastens to assert that it's not pornography. "Sex has been cheapened by porn," he told the *Times.* In Mitchell's film project, we have a prime example of what I'll call media creep.

No, that's not a term for a journalist (as in, "He's a real media creep"). It's an attempt to label a phenomenon that increasingly plagues our public space.

Here's how it works.

The sectors of the media marketplace are supposed to be seg-regated. "Adult entertainment" and "prime-time television" for example, are two separate entities, addressed to two separate au-diences. Children can watch prime-time television. They are not supposed to be able to watch porn. Likewise, cable television is supposed to have slightly different rules from those of broadcast television.

But in reality, all sectors of media compete with all other sec-tors. There is only so much time that the average audience member can devote to entertainment. After all, we have to sleep sometime, and most of us have to go to work. So in reality, broadcast television competes with cable, and prime-time tele-vision competes with video games, and mainstream Hollywood movies compete with porn, each sector scrambling after the elusive consumer.

What this means is that all forms of media inevitably "creep" toward one another. They begin to resemble one another in theme and content. As cable television becomes more and more sexually explicit, broadcast television is drawn the same way, un-til suddenly Andy Sipowitz's naked posterior is featured on *NYPD Blue* in prime time.

Independent film competes with porn until it begins to resem-ble porn. NBC inches toward HBO. Borders and barriers, which are supposed to be clear, prove themselves to be all too perme-able. We find ourselves repeatedly doing what a friend of mind calls "the parent's tomahawk chop" in front of our children's eyes, the blade of our hand acting as a barrier when other barri-ers fail.

Media creep.

The movie theater has always been a prime source of media creep. Films busted out of the Hayes Code doldrums in the 1960s, at times using sex and nudity as artistic grace notes, and at times mindlessly putting titillation on screen. It took television a few decades to answer this competitive threat, but the creep was inexorable.

Born of film's newfound permissiveness was the rating system of the Motion Picture Association of America (MPAA). Two landmark films triggered the abandonment of the old Hayes Code "Seal of Approval" system: *Who's Afraid of Virginia Woolf?*, with language such as "screw" and "hump the hostess," and *Blow Up,* an Italian import with copious amounts of nudity.

In November 1968, the MPAA system began with four simple categories: G, M (for "mature"), R, and X. The X rating, put in place at the request of theater owners, was supposedly based on the fact that a Roman child had to be age ten (X in Roman numerals) before he would be admitted to the Colosseum. The tame-by-today's-standards *Midnight Cowboy,* 1969's best-picture Oscar winner, was originally rated X.

The specific rating categories have been adjusted over the years. PG-13 was added in 1984, under the prodding of Stephen Spielberg, who complained that movies for tots and films for teens had been lumped in the same PG category. In 1990, NC-17 replaced X, which had been co-opted by porn.

Overall, the MPAA movie ratings continue to be the most successful of all content-labeling systems. How do you rate a rating system? By familiarity and ease of use. Over two-thirds of the

American public agree that MPAA ratings influence their moviegoing choices.

But the film ratings themselves have been plagued by a form of media creep, in this case labeled "ratings creep." A recent Harvard School of Public Health study quantified what many parents intuitively understood to be true. In the last decade, the ratings have allowed much more sex and profanity in PG, PG-13, and R-rated films.

"Today's PG-13 movies are approaching what the R movies looked like in 1992," study coauthor Kimberly Thompson stated. "Today's PG is approaching what PG-13 looked like a decade ago."

To cite just one example, the 1994 movie *The Santa Clause* was rated PG, while its 2002 sequel, with an equivalent amount of profanity, sexual references, and violence, was rated G.

Well, okay, tastes change and boundaries shift. But whose tastes, and whose boundaries? Polls show that parents are more uneasy than ever about sex and violence in the media. So it is Hollywood's boundaries that are shifting, not America's. It represents a particularly pernicious form of bait-and-switch to take your young child to a G movie and instead be shown a PG.

There's another "creep" afflicting us, and this one hits not media but consumers. "Porn creep" is a well-recognized psychological phenomenon whereby consumers of pornography escalate the sex-and-kinkiness quotient of the smut that they watch, download, or buy. There is something pathetic about the libido's tireless search for novelty in an area of human existence where there famously is nothing new under the sun.

Photos lead to videos, which lead to live-action Web sites. Vanilla sexual tastes bleed into fetishism and S/M. The search is endless and finally fruitless. It is said that the male predilection for channel surfing is subconsciously motivated by the idea that somewhere, on some channel, there is a naked woman dancing.

Movies have their own version of porn creep, with smut becoming more and more an accepted thematic element in mainstream films and television. In the mid-1990s, the awful *Showgirls* and the excellent *Boogie Nights* kicked off the porn-themed trend. A disturbing aspect of the latter was that star Mark Wahlberg, fresh from his teen idol status as a singer, went in this film directly into channeling porn star John Holmes. It made you wonder if he was bringing his teen fans along for the ride.

The trend continues today: the theatrically released film *The Girl Next Door* introduced a porn star neighbor as a love interest for a teenaged boy; Showtime's *Family Business* featured a hero trying to make it in smut, and Fox's *Skin* also had a smut mogul as a major character. One Internet search engine lists 250 recent films with porn as a plot element.

Porn creep, ratings creep, media creep. It's happening not only at the movies but also in television, on billboards, even in the bookstores. One way or another, America is getting thoroughly creeped out.

PART THREE

WHY WE ARE WHERE WE ARE

CHAPTER TWENTY-ONE

■ ■ ■

THE CURSE OF THE CHATTERING CLASS

WIDESPREAD DISCOMFORT, WIDESPREAD PARALYSIS.

Why is this? If there is general agreement among the Disturbed Six-in-Tenners that the tone of our culture has somehow become too trashy, why can't we adjust that tone to be more in line with our attitudes?

The answer partly lies in the existence of a group of people who dominate all political, legal, and social discourse in this country. These folks hold stubbornly to a set of beliefs that might as well be chiseled in stone, and they determine what America reads, watches, and hears.

The Chattering Class. The idea of a separate class of wordsmiths gained currency in the early 1980s, but the term itself has been around for years. I first heard it used by Jerry Brown, a.k.a. Edmund G. Brown Jr., former governor of California (Governor Moonbeam, they used to call him, for his sometimes loopy ways). Brown's now mayor of Oakland, but back during his governorship, he used the term "the Chattering Class" to sneer at the reporters, critics, and commentators who were nipping at his flanks.

"I don't know why you guys are complaining," Brown said. "The Chattering Class has it pretty good. You make good money and have comfortable jobs. It's the guy who's trying to raise a family and make ends meet who's having trouble."

There are quite a few other terms tossed around to label this same group of people. "Media elites," of course, is one that has a lot of currency nowadays. Others I've heard include "the chatterati," "the creative community," "the professional-managerial class," and "symbol manipulators."

All writers, journalists, and commentators belong to the Chattering Class. So do all publishers, editors, and publicists. Lawyers, too, since the law is most definitely a realm of the word. Hollywood is an enclave of the Chattering Class.

I am a member of this group. I am, by registering my disgust at the tone of the culture, a traitor to my class. Although at various times in my life I have done factory work, milked cows, and waited tables, for the bulk of my adult years I have earned my living by convincing others of my superior word-shuffling skills.

Let's take a step back and examine the Chattering Class, which sits atop the rest of society (to use Bob Dylan's memorable image) "like a mattress sits on a bottle of wine."

The Chattering Class is one reason why this country is successful, interesting, and a great place to live. The Chattering Class tells us our collective bedtime stories and comes up with our punch lines. It soothes us in times of trouble, entertains us with an almost antic energy, and provides meaning and depth to our lives. To use the parlance of the day, it constructs our narratives.

For members of the Chattering Class, the sanctity of free speech is an unshakable article of faith. It would be hard to over-estimate the obduracy of this belief. It's part of what defines the Chattering Class. It's the price of membership.

This makes perfect sense. We're a group of people who liter-ally live by the word, so we are naturally a tad sensitive about any sort of limits placed on speech. We tend to interpret that as an assault on our way of making a living.

In the mid-1970s I wandered into a tavern frequented by au-toworkers in Kenosha, Wisconsin, where I initiated a discussion about free trade (this was in my young and stupid days). Detroit, as well as Kenosha, Wisconsin, was getting the stuffing kicked out of it by Japan during that time, and let's just say my well-meaning rhetorical queries about the ultimate benefits of open markets and elimination of tariffs didn't go down very well. I was lucky to escape with my life.

Go ahead. Head to Youngstown, Ohio, and get into a conver-sation about steel dumping. Or talk to a Maine trawler captain about fishing quotas. Ask a dairy farmer about price supports.

It won't be a calm discussion.

When people feel their livelihoods are threatened, a brand of rising hysteria enters their argument. Any threat, no matter how abstract, is greeted with an anger all out of proportion to the ac-tual risk.

Talk about freedom of expression with a member of the Chat-tering Class and you'll see the same primordial, from-the-gut reaction. We deal in words, so any talk about placing limits on words becomes extremely emotional.

The difference between the member of the Chattering Class and the steelworker, dairy farmer, or fisherman is that we have managed to dress up our vocational hysteria in exalted, quasi-religious garments. The Chattering Class regularly wraps itself in the cloak of the First Amendment. The source of the anxiety might be the same as for the farmer, fisherman, or roughneck, but the strategy of response is far more grandiose.

"I'm a First Amendment absolutist." I used to say this all the time. It wasn't true, of course. The First Amendment's guarantees of free speech are not absolute at all. They have asterisks, exceptions, and quid pro quos stickered all over them. Obscenity is one exception; "fighting words" is another.

The Chattering Class has defined the debate over free expression in its own terms. Those terms are strict to the point of rigid. Any proposed encroachment on the Chattering Class's absolute right to say, howl, rant, or bellow whatever enters its fervid mind is greeted with instant and frantic rejection.

"Censor!"

This always reminds me of the pigeon in *Alice's Adventures in Wonderland,* who confronts an elongated Alice invading her nest with shrieks of "Serpent! Serpent! Ser-PENT!"

Alice tries patiently to explain that she's not a serpent, but nothing will satisfy the pigeon.

"As if it wasn't trouble enough hatching the eggs," said the Pigeon; "but I must be on the look-out for serpents night and day!"

As if it wasn't trouble enough writing books . . . or making films . . . or producing pop songs . . .

Censor! Censor! Cen-SOR!

It's the war cry of the Chattering Class.

When the rock singer Bono used an expletive at the televised Golden Globes ceremony, describing an act as "[bleeping] brilliant," the Chattering Class rallied around. The Screen Actors Guild, Viacom, CBS, NBC (which broadcast the ceremony), and twenty other media organizations filed a petition with the FCC defending the rock star.

There are plenty of people who don't just want to support Bono—they want to *be* Bono. Those cool blue shades, the humanitarian work, the songs . . . He just may be at the apex of the Chattering Class hierarchy.

The Chattering Class lives in a stark, us-versus-them world. On one side are the Philistines, the prudes, the puritans, the fingershakers, Anthony Comstock and Carrie Nation and self-consciously moral hypocrites like Jimmy Swaggart and Jim Bakker. Lumped on that side, too, are the soccer moms and suburban dads of the workaday world.

Ranged on the opposite side are the champions of freedom, crusaders for the rights of humankind, acidly funny misfits like H. L. Mencken, Allen Ginsberg, Lenny Bruce, and Howard Stern. On that side is the rock star Bono. Who among the Chattering Class wants to be caught dead on the other side of Bono?

Nobody, not even the Pope. Especially if you are, deep down, just a teensy bit insecure about your status in the realm of cool.

Because the Chattering Class has managed to make this all about the cool versus the uncool.

As far as the Chattering Class is concerned, the line to be drawn has nothing to do with boundaries of taste, decorum, or moderation. The real line is one of the most brutal, unforgiving, and shape-shifting lines of all, the line between cool and uncool. Hard to believe, but this is the boundary that I've seen drawn again and again by my friends in the Chattering Class. It represents our true allegiance, beyond God and country and, to some degree, beyond self. I know people who would rather die than be seen wearing the wrong brand of blue jeans.

But let's lift the question out of the realm of personal insecurities for a moment. Isn't one of the bedrock foundations of American democracy, of every one of the world's major religions, of liberalism and compassionate conservatism actually the same concept?

For the weak, and against the strong.

If you look past the cool and uncool dichotomy that the Chattering Class has wrapped itself up in, you can see the debate over the cultural content of our society in exactly those terms.

The very young, of course, are always the weakest members of any community, relying on others for their sustenance and well-being as well as for their voice. In this country, too, the overtly religious, the decorous, the modest and easily offended people among us have been effectively marginalized, weakened to the point of invisibility in our stampede to create an all-sex, all-the-time culture.

Who speaks for the very young and the wholly marginalized

against the forces that seek to hypersexualize our culture? Against massive combinations of profit that have built billion-dollar industries using human sexuality as their tool?

On which side of the line do you want to be?

For the weak, and against the strong.

Bono's down for that, and we should be, too.

■ ■ ■

CHAPTER TWENTY-TWO

THE MALE ANIMAL

THERE ARE A LOT OF TIMES I FEEL MY BUTTONS BEING PUSHED in the current cultural climate, as though I'm being poked and prodded by forces unseen.

"It's pretty easy to pull your chain, because you're *all* chain," my wife tells me.

But I don't think so. I've managed to prize myself at least a little bit out of my sheltered midwestern origins. As far as sexually explicit material goes, I experienced whatever New York City could throw at me in the pre-AIDS early 1980s, which is saying a good deal. We used to joke that because God did not rain fire and brimstone down on Manhattan back then, destroying it to the last grain of sand, apologies were due to Sodom and Gomorrah, because we thought we outdid them.

So I'm not a prude, or a provincial, or a puritan. But a lot of us feel our buttons are being pushed nowadays, and there's a good reason for that.

They are.

Much of the cultural content circulating today is created by twentysomething males. The publishers, producers, and moguls might be silver-haired silverbacks, lying about being on the young side of fifty, but the people they hire, the people who do their work for them are almost invariably postadolescent males.

PAMs. That's what we used to call them, back at *Screw.* Postadolescent males. A marketing consultant gave us a presentation one day, solemnly calling our attention to PAMs as our target audience, the consumers to whom we supposedly pitched our message. (This consultant later happened to turn out to be an embezzler. Goldstein had an almost uncanny knack for employing embezzlers. There were three or four I recall in the period I wrote for him.)

That concept of the PAM always stuck with me. As well as being prime purveyors of the porn sensibility, PAMs are prime purchasers of the stuff. And of course, PAMs are all over the media.

I know whereof I speak. I've been in those shops full of ink-stained wretches, in magazine offices, in smut companies, in Hollywood studios, or in editorial departments of big book publishers. Sure, there was always a smattering of females. But to a greater or lesser degree (greater in the realm of smut, lesser in the realm of book publishing, with magazines falling somewhere in between), PAMs predominated. And more than that, PAMs set the tone for the enterprises.

And a snarky, aggressive tone it is. When I first started working at *Screw,* one of its editors was Josh Friedman, a PAM so enthusiastic about smut that he seemed to devote much of his life to it. Friedman haunted the pre-Disney Times Square of the 1980s, and wrote a cult-favorite book about its topless shoeshine parlors, live-sex shows, and small-time street hustlers. After Times Square was revitalized in the 1990s, the neighborhood lost its Nelson Algren–style charm for Josh. He preferred it smutty.

Friedman was a strapping, handsome guy, an extremely talented writer and, from his unlikely perch at *Screw* magazine, a sardonic commentator on the American cultural landscape.

Josh and his brother, the talented political cartoonist Drew Friedman, collaborated on a series of graphic comics, collected together in books, which poked fun at celebrities—zeroing in on the feminine voice of Wayne Newton, for example, or the lousy dentistry of Rolling Stone Keith Richards. They were precursors of the kind of famicide so much in vogue today.

The Friedmans were born to the Chattering Class. Their father, Bruce Jay Friedman, was among the top playwrights and screenwriters of the day who wrote, among his many other credits, the movie *Splash!, Stir Crazy,* the Richard Pryor–Gene Wilder smash, and the hit play *Steambath.* This latter stands as the first dramatic production in which a woman purposefully bared her breasts on national television, when Valerie Perrine appeared in a PBS version of the play in 1973.

Josh Friedman was a smoldering presence in the *Screw* offices, extremely likable, but with an edge of violence that always seemed inexplicable to me. I never could figure out what he was so angry about. I would have paid to have his life. Women adored him. But his anger came out in the texts he wrote for the Fried-

man Brothers comics, venomous lampoons of the rich and famous. It also came out in his work for *Screw*.

"I want to do the world's most disgusting coverline," Friedman
announced one morning, referring to the large-print lettering on
the front cover of the magazine. Coverlines usually announce the
contents of the publication, but in *Screw*'s case, they were only
tangentially related to what was inside.

"I just walked past a newsstand," Friedman said. "I saw this
secretary, you know, panty hose up to here, perfect hairdo."

"Probably from Brooklyn," I said.

"Or Queens," Josh agreed. "I thought of her, you know, coming up the newsstand to buy her morning *Daily News*, or maybe
some breath mints, and she has to reach across a whole stack of
Screw magazines."

He laughed at the image. I laughed at the image. We began
tossing out coverlines that our Typical Secretary would happen
to read, trying to come up with one that would upset her so much
she wouldn't be able to think of anything for the rest of the day.

That's how we all thought. We weren't shy about articulating
it, either. "Maybe we could come up with one that would make
her throw up," Friedman said, laughing.

We began to laugh uproariously as each new suggestion
topped the last. Each one was grosser, fouler, more outrageous.
We were mad scientists. The unsuspecting secretary would be
our guinea pig.

When *Screw* hit the newsstands the next week, it carried the
intentionally disturbing coverline "Special Sex and Diarrhea

Issue!" That was the best we could come up with. Our pièce de résistance.

We even stood around the corner newsstand for a while the morning the issue came out, hoping that our fantasy would come true, and we would gleefully witness Miss Typical Secretary glance down, read the *Screw* coverline, and stagger away in horror, her life changed forever.

Nothing happened. No one cared not even a tiny bit what appeared on the cover of *Screw* magazine. We gave up and trudged back to the office, our visions of grandeur faded.

I count Friedman as a good friend of mine, and it pains me to hold him up as an example, but I only mention him in the context of a mea culpa of my own. Looking back at that "world's most disgusting coverline" incident now, I can't help but second-guess my motives.

Why did I care what some secretary I had never met before thought or experienced or felt? Why did I want to ruin her day? The whole impulse now strikes me as not funny but as lame, revealing the tight little bundle of social insecurity I was back then.

Our delusions lent us a power we didn't otherwise have. "What is exhilarating in bad taste," writes the French poet Baudelaire, "is the aristocratic pleasure of giving offense."

PAMs do the grunt work not only for smut rags but also for mainstream magazines, on sitcom writing staffs, in MTV studios, and with advertising copywriting. America has basically handed over the keys to its culture to the PAM, saying, "Here you are, kid, take it for a spin around the block." Then we respond with hurt and anger when the run-amok car plunges into our homes.

Do you find a particular aspect of the media offensive? Have you been culture-whipped? Have you inadvertently run across an objectionable piece of smut while you were minding your own business, trying to get through your day?

A PAM was probably to blame. The thing to remember is that you were *supposed* to be offended. PAMs absolutely delight in offending others. It's one of the only ways they have of relating to other people. In other societies, all this offensive energy is bottled up, expended on the playing field, or just ignored. Only in America have we enshrined it as the central quality of our culture.

■ ■ ■

CHILLING SLOPES AND
SLIPPERY EFFECTS

A PLAGUE ON BOTH YOUR HOUSES. THE ISSUE OF SEXUAL expression in America is so polarized that anyone who claims the middle ground is likely to be caught in a crossfire from both sides. From the left, a steel-jacketed enfilade about free expression. From the right, salvos about filth, sleaze, and degradation.

The issue is politicized to within an inch of its life. The debate becomes a contest to see which can scare more people—the bugaboo of censorship, or the monster of pornography. It is axiomatic that politics is compromise, but no one is much interested in that here. They are too busy honing their rhetoric.

Maybe what we should do is look left, look right, conclude they're both nuts, and calmly but firmly insist on the obvious.

Yes, there must be boundaries on sexual expression. And no, the effort to set boundaries can't extend to eliminating the smut that so many Americans purchase, view, and enjoy.

Of course, that's not going to please anyone, on the left or the

154

right. "The only viable solution," said the writer Amos Oz about the Palestinian-Israeli conflict, "is the one that makes everyone unhappy."

Let's circle back to the fact that most people out there, those Disturbed Six-in-Tenners, are extremely uneasy about the amount of explicit sexuality, soft-core smut, and indecent innuendo they have to wade through just to get through their day-to-day lives. You may quibble and pull apart poll results all you want. But rarely does that big a chunk of the American populace agree about anything. We might want to commemorate the occasion by actually doing something about it.

I don't want six out of ten of my neighbors going around "very disturbed" about anything. It offends my egalitarian principles. Such widespread unhappiness means that something is not right in Whoville. Besides, some of these people own weapons.

You would think as a community that we would be responsive to such a common concern, but we're not. The situation continues, people remain frustrated, year after year. The Chattering Class basically says "Sorry," to the Six-in-Ten. Actually, it doesn't even say "Sorry." It says "Tough," adding, barely under its breath, "You neo-Puritan Philistine weenie."

Not quite neighborly, is it?

Parents are the Rodney Dangerfields of the political left. They are sneeringly described as "breeders" and lumped with that whole bourgeois/suburban/workaday nexus that is antiart, antifreedom, antihip. The concerns of parents trying to raise children are dismissed condescendingly.

We have been here before, and that's part of the reason we are where we are now. The first two or three decades of the last century saw the dismantling of communal standards of decency and reticence that had bound this country together since its inception.

Here's a thumbnail: For thousands of years previous to the modern age, those areas of life where the human being is reduced to a purely physical level have been taboo. "It has always been the bodily part of human existence that needed to be hidden in privacy, all things connected to the life process itself," writes Hannah Arendt in *The Human Condition*.

At the end of the nineteenth century, anthropological research confirmed this. In every society, "sexual activities, sleep and excretion are surrounded by protective taboos and mechanisms of concealment and isolation," observes the influential British anthropologist Bronislaw Malinowski.

But a mere three decades later, by 1930, that ideal of privacy had already begun to be dismantled. This represented a turning upside down of everything it had meant to be human since history began.

In quick order at the dawn of the twentieth century, several forces and developments worked a thoroughgoing social transformation. Journalists of the penny press trained the public glare on the private lives of celebrities, politicians, and entertainers. Reformers argued that privacy shrouded social evils such as abuse, alcoholism, and enslavement. And new realist writers sought to remove barriers of privacy to present the intimate lives of their characters.

Finally, in the 1930s, the popularization of Freudian psychology performed the coup de grâce on the ideal of privacy. In the

Freudian worldview, what privacy really meant was that you were hiding something. Suppression was sick, evil. Unburdening, exposing oneself, was liberating, praiseworthy.

Some of this answered to the Everyman dynamic of a new age. We all have bodies. Those who seek to hide their bodily functions in private, because of modesty or refinement, were now seen as somehow denying the physical equality of being human. In a democratic society, there was something suspiciously aristocratic about modesty, decorum, and taste.

Anthony Comstock was a self-appointed censor who held America in the grip of his personal version of morality for over forty years, from the 1870s through the early 1900s, over much of the period we are talking about. At first, Comstock's activities, confiscating what he deemed to be unseemly materials in the mails, were seen as good and necessary.

But the age changed. By the end of his reign as America's chief censor, Comstock was characterized as a hysterical fraud, so much in terror of his own sexual demons that he sought to stamp sexuality completely out of the public world.

This model of a censor endures to this day: a sick individual, hiding something, who presents a hypocritical face of morality to the world. It is the model subscribed to by such progressive advocacy groups as the ACLU Arts Censorship Project, the Freedom Forum, and the Free Expression Clearinghouse.

These groups have developed marvelous mechanisms with which to answer what they perceive to be threats to free speech. And though these might be deeply held beliefs by individuals with pristine intentions, in the real world they function to cut off all discussion about the out-of-control sexual content of today's popular culture.

Any effort, no matter how modest, to establish boundaries in public expression is greeted with a shriek. "That's a slippery slope!" these advocates declare, implying that any step in that direction leads inevitably to book burning in the public square. Thus that first step becomes *equivalent* to book burning in the public square.

It's a strange, disjointed experience. You think you are talking about using filters on Internet terminals in public libraries, but the ground shifts under you, and suddenly you are arguing about book burning in the public square.

Slippery slope, slippery slope, slippery SLOPE!

I guess you could see a lot of things that way. Child labor laws are the first step on the slippery slope that leads to government control of the workplace. Yes-sss, I guess, but I also guess I'll remain in favor of child labor laws, thank you very much.

Artists are coddled creatures. Any whiff of cold air in their direction curls them up like orchids in a spring frost. This is the "chilling-effect argument," which paints an equally dire picture to that of the slippery slope.

The chilling-effect argument runs along these lines: At the first hint of boundaries placed on expression, artists and writers will internalize those boundaries. They are no longer free as the wind blows, free as the grass grows. The chilling effect will chill them right out of whatever masterpiece they were contemplating.

But the truth is, writers and artists always work within boundaries. To suggest otherwise is mere Chattering Class megalomania. It is interesting to recall that Tolstoy wrote in an age that required strict boundaries on free expression. As did Mark Twain, for that matter. Film aesthetes might clamor against the film-rating system as "censorship," but the very films they most revere were produced under rigorous standards of decency.

A good example of the Chattering Class's contortions of logic on the issue of sex in the media comes in the "harm-to-minors" debate. One of the major arguments for setting boundaries on sexual content has always been to protect children. But in the stark, black-and-white world of the Chattering Class, all arguments, even those that seem to state self-evident facts, must be answered. So a counterargument has arisen, attempting to convince us that exposure to sexually charged images does no essential harm to children.

This whole line of thought strikes me as laughably wrong-headed, but whole books have been written to back it up. *Not in Front of the Children,* by Marjorie Heins, examines pertinent research. The social sciences are evidently in the midst of a tug-of-war debate over smut's impact on children. In *Harmful to Minors,* the journalist Judith Levine argues that efforts to limit exposure to smut actually wind up harming children in the long run.

I guarantee that no one in his or her right mind pays the least attention to the sophistries contained in these books. They resemble a brave and nimble thinker arguing decisively that we should all place our hands on a hot stove, that the burn will heal, that we shouldn't get upset about it.

The American Academy of Pediatrics recently completed a

study showing that children who view a lot of sexually explicit content on television tend to have sex earlier. No doubt we'll soon see a Chattering Class response arguing that losing one's virginity in junior high is a good thing.

The Chattering Class has a chip on its shoulder about children, and a chip on the shoulder, my grandmother was fond of reminding me, means that there's wood up above. When *Desperate Housewives* actress Nicollette Sheridan dropped towel in a teaser intro to ABC's Monday Night Football, *The New York Times*'s Frank Rich was point man for the effort to dismiss concerns over dorsal nudity on prime time.

Rich kicked off his *Times* column with dripping sarcasm: "Oh, the poor, suffering little children." He cast a cold eye on the idea that a child might have been harmed by such a violation of cultural taboos. Quite rightfully, the left wears its heart on its sleeve when it comes to starving and abused children. Imagine Rich, writing sarcastically about the Sudan, "Oh, the poor, suffering little children." But he seems aggressively willing to allow the politically weakest members of the culture be exposed to its crudest excesses.

What is happening here? Why is there such a blind spot in the compassionate liberalism of the Chattering Class? I suspect that on a personal level, Frank Rich and others like him sympathize with the idea that perhaps young children shouldn't be plopped down in front of hard-core sex videos, say. But politically, which is to say rhetorically, they are not allowed even to whisper these personal misgivings. It must be difficult for them, this tension between private belief and public utterance. It's a wonder they don't explode. Oh, the poor, suffering little commentators.

What these folks don't seem to get is that protecting children from smut involves a values-based decision, not much influenced by political commentary or social research. It doesn't matter how many books on the subject I read. After finishing one that devotes 350 pages to the proposition that smut is pretty much innocuous, my response is a heartfelt "whatever."

Then I go ahead and do what I have always done, which is attempt to patrol the boundaries of my daughter's world.

Is this a case of "Don't confuse me with the facts"? I don't think so. No matter how many books are written, no matter how many statistics are marshaled, on a very primal level it doesn't feel right to have my child exposed to explicit sexual imagery.

But the free-expression folks have got us boxed in. Any proposal to get more choice into the process of who sees what is met with well-practiced rejection. All counterarguments have been effectively checkmated.

Go ahead. Raise the issue of taste, civility, decorum with these people.

"Taste is just one powerful group of people imposing their opinions on less powerful group of people. It's all about power."

So runs their line of reasoning. Here's the real thing, from a 1996 ACLU position paper ("Popular Music Under Siege") against music labeling: "Clearly, the real intention of the would-be music censors is to impose on all Americans the tastes and values of political powerbrokers who don't connect with the experiences and concerns of the young, the alienated and minorities."

There is something wrong here. Taste and appropriate behavior are universal concepts, at play in every society—even if the particulars vary from culture to culture. Those communities of "the young, the alienated and minorities"? They also have standards of the appropriate.

Yet in our culture we have lost a way to talk about these ideas. The very words—"taste," "civility," "decorum"—have been checkmated out of our national language. We need to find a way to get them back.

I'll suggest another word to you: "cynicism." It's the belief that the worst of all possible aspects of something is also the most meaningful. "America is a brutish imperial power." Even if you believe that sentence to be true, is that the most salient point we can make about America and its place in the world? What about this country's historic contributions to thought, culture, civilization? Dismissed by the cynic.

Likewise with the concepts of good taste, civility, decorum.

"They are merely an expression of cultural prejudices."

Even if we accept that as true, is that the most important thing we can say about these principles? How about the idea that taste expresses our yearning toward an ideal, or that civility is really a form of dedication to community, or that decorum represents our caring for the feelings of our fellow human beings?

The truth is, we have boxed ourselves in. We have allowed the arguments for free expression, worthy as they are, to deny us simple human values such as decency and taste, concepts that are integral to our enjoyment of life.

We have to be able to say a very simple sentence to ourselves: "Maybe it's not a good idea." Maybe it's not a good idea to talk about anal sex at 7:30 in the morning, maybe it's not a good idea to splay oneself naked across a billboard, maybe it's not a good idea to give every single joke a sexual edge on a prime-time sitcom, maybe it's not a good idea to mousetrap kids into a sex site with a deceptive URL, maybe it's not a good idea to drive around displaying hard-core DVD porn where others can see it.

To limit our speech out of deference to others translates, according to free-expression orthodoxy, into self-censorship, puritanism, or even fascism. There's no middle ground. We don't want to bow to the book burners, do we? Then let it all hang out!

Demonizing the ACLU doesn't help. As I said, I'm a member (all right, if I must use the phrase that helped lose Michael Dukakis the presidency, I'm a "card-carrying member"). The advocates of absolute freedom of expression have a place in any democratic society. The folks of the ACLU are there in order to do what they do, which is to represent an absolute viewpoint.

I don't think the ACLU is the enemy. Who knows—there might be a time when you or I find ourselves on the wrong side of a barbed-wire fence somewhere, and then we will be pretty thankful that such an organization exists. We can listen to the ACLU, and then politely and firmly insist that we must have a choice in what we read, see, and hear.

Likewise, I see little reason to demonize the taboo trashers among us. They are doing what they do, urged on by who knows what personal dynamic. They are not evil, or subhuman, or satanic.

The taboo is the flip side of the sacred. They represent two sides of the same coin. Because the sacred has been rooted from the lives of so many in the world today, they seek to root out its shadow opposite, too, and eliminate all taboos.

"But in the very act of violation," writes Edward Rothstein in the *Times,* "a reminder of its opposite is glimpsed. In desecration is found a recollection of the divine."

That probably puts too fine a point on what's going on in advertising, movies, music, and television today. A lot of taboo busting is just plain nasty. Its motivation is pure stick-a-finger-in-your-eye. But in a perverse, pathetic, and quite hapless manner, breaking taboos might be a way for lives impoverished of the holy to grope after it. I just wish they'd keep their groping private.

There are political realities, and then there are rhetorical realities. Rhetorical reality demands that you never give an inch. Compromise is unthinkable. Nothing ever changes in rhetorical reality, because it exists in a timeless space of eternal ideals. Rhetorical reality is especially great for scaring up funding for your advocacy organization so that you don't have to go out and get real work like everyone else.

Political reality is messy. It demands compromise. Change is the coin of the realm. I'd like to propose a simple test for those involved in the indecency debate, designed to suggest whether someone is living in political or rhetorical reality.

Check a box, "agree" or "disagree."

"There must be boundaries on public expression."

All those who check the box "disagree" are not really involved in this debate. They are rhetoricians. Their views might be interesting, or at least loud, but they have little political meaning.

A well-known (but probably apocryphal) anecdote has the playwright George Bernard Shaw asking a woman if she would go to bed with him for a hundred pounds. Indignant, the woman replied she would not. He then proposed fifty thousand pounds. Astounded by the amount, the woman paused, then said, "Perhaps." How about five pounds?

"Mister Shaw," she cried, "what kind of woman do you take me for?"

"We've already established what kind of woman you are," Shaw replied. "Now we are merely haggling over price."

No matter how liberals might respond to the litmus-test question above, virtually everyone believes in boundaries on public expression. Most people agree you can't yell "Fire!" in a crowded theater.

So we have already established that boundaries on speech have to be maintained. Now we are only haggling over where those boundaries need to be placed. And that's a political and social decision, not a rhetorical one.

CHAPTER TWENTY-FOUR

■ ■ ■

CENSOR SENSIBILITY

A PLAGUE ON BOTH YOUR HOUSES.

One reason why liberals can afford to be so dismissive of arguments in favor of establishing cultural boundaries is that their opposition on the right is so pathetic. There is no other way to look at it: censors down through the decades represent a confederacy of dunces worthy of that other bumbler's realm, the U.S. Congress.

At one time or another in this country, censors have banned works by Ernest Hemingway, James Joyce, and Vladimir Nabokov. The books they've challenged include Geoffrey Chaucer's *The Canterbury Tales,* Madeleine L'Engle's science-fiction classic *A Wrinkle in Time,* Judith Guest's *Ordinary People,* and Maya Angelou's *I Know Why the Caged Bird Sings.*

Network standards-and-decency rules long required married people to be portrayed as sleeping in twin beds on television. A pastor in Florida attacked Barney the dinosaur for being satanic.

Concerned Women for America labeled one of their current position papers with this ripped-from-the-1950s headline: "Communist Ethos Alive and Well in U.S. Cable." Jerry Falwell once
railed against *Teletubbies* for promoting gender confusion.

Let's just say the effort to regulate expression in America has
not exactly been a model of moderation. Hysteria not only
reigns, it pours.

In the early 1980s, when New York City had Al Goldstein as its
own pet pornographer, it also had its own very active antismut
crusader, the Reverend Bruce Ritter. Ritter ran the Covenant
House for homeless youths, first in Times Square and then near
the *Screw* offices in Chelsea.

Ritter was adamant about the source for all the troubles of
drug abuse, prostitution, and homelessness that he saw among
the youths to whom he ministered. Smut was the root cause of it
all, he stated repeatedly. He was particularly keen on forcing
Goldstein's cable show, *Midnight Blue,* off the air. So when Ritter was retired from Covenant House under a cloud of child sexual abuse allegations, Goldstein crowed.

No wonder censors get a bad name. And because the effort
to set boundaries on sexual content in the media is inevitably
tarred with the censorship brush, that effort has also been less
than effective.

Which is a shame, because I don't think very many of the Disturbed Six-in-Tenners want to put all expression through the sexual deflavorizer. Some of them might even choose to subscribe to
the excellent (and graphic) adult programming on premium
channels such as *The Sopranos*—which they will watch after

they've put the kids to bed. They might be "very disturbed" by rampaging sexual content in the media, but they still want their VH1. They contradict themselves. Humans are funny that way.

None of that for the quite extensive censorship advocacy industry in this country. Black or white, please, no herringbone. You are either for 'em or agin 'em.

Morality in Media (MiM) has been fighting for years to get the Federal government to enforce its own obscenity laws. Staffers are earnest but increasingly frustrated, because in this day and age, obscenity laws are unpopular. MiM has found itself out of step with large segments of the populations, out of step, I suspect, even with the Disturbed Six-In-Tenners. The advocacy group wants prosecutions, prison sentences, and you get the idea from its literature that a few electrocutions might not be a bad idea, either. A nice, fat Federal obscenity conviction, with a smut-mogul humiliated in prison stripes, might feed a need for retribution, but most people realize it won't fully address the situation.

Similarly, the otherwise quite worthy Parents Television Council (PTC) goes too far by decrying the coprolalia of basic cable television. PTC feels the need to go one step further than prime time and launch itself at all sexual expression on the tube, no matter if it is presented in programs that clearly have artistic merit, or are on premium services such as HBO.

I am a big fan of such HBO-produced programs as *The Sopranos, Six Feet Under, The Wire,* and *Deadwood.* The language in these shows can be profane in the extreme. Their portrayals of sex are oftentimes raw and graphic. But I believe the human drama on display is among the highest produced in American culture today.

HBO is a premium cable service. It is a choice consumers consciously must make. I pay to have it pumped into my home. My exposure to its sexual content is never inadvertent or involuntary. My wife and I are careful not to expose our daughter to material she is too young to understand.

A lock-'em-up, zero-tolerance approach to smut won't work, first of all, and will never garner a consensus in a society that values free speech. Groups such as Concerned Women for America, American Family Association (AFA) and Focus on the Family are passionate advocates for a world that has pretty much disappeared. MiM got its start in 1962, the AFA is over 25 years old, while Focus on the Family just passed its second decade, but sexually explicit content in the media has exploded over the same period of time. They have been prophets crying in the wilderness.

In order to be truly effective, we've got to take measures that will appeal to the Six-in-Tenners.

All right, another litmus-test question, to gauge whether someone is merely interested in rhetorical reality or can deal with political compromise.

Check the box, "agree" or "disagree."

"Sexually explicit material is purchased and enjoyed by a huge number of people in the United States and should be available to all adults who want it."

The rhetoricians of the right might have trouble choking this down. They may be more interested in fund-raising than in actual social change. But again, the stakes are high enough here to require sacrifices from everyone, including the sacrifice of compromise.

Mark Twain used to talk about "the calm confidence of a Christian with four aces." Passion and certitude haven't been enough to get the job done for true believers such as Donald Wildmon of the AFA or Bob Peters of MIM. A spirit of negotiation, conciliation, and political realism just might have to be their ace in the hole.

The real truth is that the flood of smut in our culture comes from sources all across the political spectrum, left and right, liberal and conservative.

"The rest of the country looks upon New York like we're left-wing Communist, Jewish, homosexual pornographers," says Woody Allen in *Annie Hall*. "I think of us that way, sometimes, and I live here."

That's the classic profile of the purveyor of smut: Al Goldstein. But the stereotypes don't hold true. Rupert Murdoch, who owns News Corporation, has impeccable conservative credentials. Yet his Fox network has consistently struck new lows in televised indecency. The FCC hit Murdoch's Fox network with the highest-ever proposed fine for indecency, $1.2 million for its short-lived show, *Married by America*. *Married . . . With Children,* one of the Fox network's first hit shows, was actually the we're-mad-as-hell-and-we-aren't-going-to-take-it-anymore trigger that brought the Parents Television Council into being. Vincent Gallo, the film director who erected the oral-sex billboard over Sunset Strip, is a staunch Republican.

Likewise, censorship doesn't always cleave neatly along right-left lines. *Huckleberry Finn* has long been the target of otherwise extremely liberal activists, who have also led the charge against hate speech. And right-wing icon Rush Limbaugh has problems with the recent indecency initiative by the FCC.

"I'm in the free-speech business, and indecency could be defined any number of ways, depending on who's in power," Limbaugh told *Time* magazine. "So it's a red flag to me. I am always concerned about it."

■ ■ ■

WHY OBSCENITY PROSECUTION
DOESN'T WORK

THE CURRENT LEGAL DEFINITION OF OBSCENITY HAS SURVIVED pretty much intact for over three decades, since the Supreme Court's 1973 decision in *Miller* v. *California.* Since that time, smut has exploded in ways that back then weren't even a gleam in a pornographer's eye. Clearly, there is some intrinsic problem with the prosecution of obscenity. It hasn't been able stem the tide.

There are a couple concepts useful to remember here. Obscenity is a legal term. Even though a lot of people—especially those who favor tighter restrictions on sexually oriented speech—make the rhetorical leap of "pornography = obscenity," or even "sex = obscenity," it is not necessarily true. A lot of smut isn't obscene. Or rather, only smut that has been determined in a court of law to violate obscenity statutes is obscene. This represents a tiny fraction of what's out there.

Three standards must be met before material can be found obscene in court: prurience, offensiveness, and lack of merit.

172

That's the Cliff's Notes version, of course, and a lot of trees have died so that lawyers can argue voluminously in print over each element of this three-pronged test. Basically, though, to be obscene the speech in question has to turn you on ("prurience") and also, paradoxically, turn you off ("offensiveness"). It also must be totally lacking in artistic, literary, or pretty much any other kind of redeeming quality.

Who decides? Juries decide. How do they decide? Well, they must apply "community standards" to determine if the material in question—words, images, or any other kind of speech—meets the three tests for obscenity. Community standards were what Ogden Nash was thinking of when he wrote this 1931 ditty:

> Senator Smoot (Republican, Ut.)
> Is planning a ban on smut
> Oh rooti-ti-toot for Smoot of Ut.
> And his reverent occiput.
> Smite, Smoot, smite for Ut.,
> Grit your molars and do your dut.,
> Gird up your l—ns,
> Smite h-p and th-gh,
> We'll all be Kansas
> By and By.

The problem nowadays, of course, is that not even Kansas is allowed to be Kansas anymore. Whether they want to or not, and no matter what Senator Smoot seems to do or say, Kansans must endure the same barrage of smut as the rest of the country.

If and when a jury jumps through the hoops to decide that the specific material meets the three-pronged test as determined by community standards, the government can act. Obscene speech has no legal protection under the First Amendment's free-speech guarantees. Courts can freely penalize the producer of such speech without running afoul of the Constitution.

So? What's the government waiting for? Why aren't obscenity trials as plentiful as adult Web pages? Even under the get-tough Bush-Ashcroft administration, there were only twenty-one obscenity convictions for the years 2000–04. That total seems puny beside figures like 260 million porn Web pages, or eight hundred million annual X-rated video and DVD rentals, or an adult entertainment market worth ten billion dollars a year.

No matter what political stripe U.S. attorneys wear, they are members of the Chattering Class, in that they make their living in the realm of the word. I don't care who you are, if you are a member of the Chattering Class, there is a psychological obstacle to get over before you wade in to block speech. If you prosecute a homicide charge, then you have the satisfaction of putting away a murderer. If you prosecute an obscenity charge, yes, you have the satisfaction of putting away a smut mogul, but you also render yourself vulnerable to charges of being a censor. Bono might not want to shake your hand.

Obscenity prosecutions are onerous, expensive, never a slam dunk. They are open to political suasion and partisan crossfire. No wonder prosecutors hesitate. We have gone through eras with more than a few obscenity prosecutions (the second term of

Ronald Reagan—remember the Meese Commission?) and we have gone through periods with very few (the 1990s, and the period after September 11, 2001). The number of obscenity prosecutions has had little impact on the availability of smut.

Obscenity is a precision instrument, like a scalpel, sharpened on the whetstone of politics, when what we need in order to preserve our public commons is something more akin to an earthmover. We need to segregate smut so that people who wish not to be confronted by it are not. And we need to recognize that people who don't necessarily want it shoved in their faces might at times want to consume it privately.

There is abundant indication that our community values have shifted in the past twenty-five years. If nothing else, the American public has voted with its pocketbooks. The next U.S. attorney who steps into a federal courtroom to prosecute an obscenity charge is going to have to answer the following conundrum: when a community (the American public) pours ten billion dollars a year into an industry, can that industry reasonably be portrayed as violating community standards?

It's a killing contradiction, and it's only going to get worse. There is both anecdotal and statistical evidence to support the idea that tolerance of smut in the under-thirty generation is reaching some sort of critical mass. Half of eighteen- to twenty-nine-year-olds answered "yes" when polled if they had seen an X-rated movie in the last year.

"[Smut has] become popular, cool, acceptable in this 18-to-25 age group," Luke Ford, who writes an Internet gossip column on porn stars, told *60 Minutes.* "My age group—I'm 37—my age group and up, we think porn is something that's shameful. But for kids half my age, they think it's cool."

The mainstreaming of smut by TV and publishing produces an effect on younger and younger audiences. "When I was hanging out with Jenna," *How to Make Love Like a Porn Star* coauthor Neil Strauss told *Time Out* New York, "she would be approached by all these twelve-year-old girls and their mothers. It was always a mob scene. The girls had seen her on *E! True Hollywood Story* and would ask her to take photographs with them. The kids treated her like she was [pop-music star] Avril Lavigne." Obscenity prosecution won't go away. But it is increasingly a political tool, not a social one. Because it has nothing to do with indecency, it won't really address the issue of our public space being overwhelmed by multiple barrages of sex from TV, the Internet, advertising, and movies.

The one aspect of legal obscenity that might help patrol the boundaries at least of our children's world is the law as it pertains to minors. Two U.S. Supreme Court rulings are germane: in *Butler* v. *Michigan,* the court ruled that adults could not be limited to what is suitable for children; and in *Ginsberg* v. *New York,* it held that some material not obscene for adults is nonetheless obscene for children.

Ginsberg hasn't assumed a central place in U.S. jurisprudence. There hasn't been a single prosecution under its "obscene to minors" provision. But it is still the law of the land.

What the Court was saying in *Ginsberg* is that there is a variable definition of obscenity, one very different for minors than the one that applies to adults. This could have vast implications to the world of the Internet, where children and adults tend to be thrown into the same mix, helter-skelter, bumping up against the same sexually explicit content, inadvertently or not.

Again, the Supreme Court rulings in *Butler* and *Ginsberg* make it clear. Adults can't be treated as children under obscenity law, but children aren't to be treated as adults, either.

How would this concept of variable obscenity work on the Internet, for example? All areas of the Web open to children would have to be cleansed of sexual content—not judged by adult obscenity standards, but by the more stringent "obscene to minors" ruling established by the Supreme Court. That means even casual nudity would be actionable, provided a child could access it intentionally or blunder on it inadvertently.

But areas of the Internet closed to minors—guarded by use of a credit card, for example, or by already well established online age verification technologies—could not be policed by obscenity standards tailored for children. It's a two-tier approach, and it is the only use of legal obscenity that might have a measurable impact on the amount of sexually explicit material jamming up the public commons.

Much of the smut readily available on the Web probably meets this "obscene to minors" standard. But remember: you stating that something is obscene, me stating that something is obscene, even the attorney general stating that something is obscene is just talk. The only folks who can decide whether something is obscene sit on a jury.

Obscenity has nothing to say about Janet Jackson's nipple,

about neathage on billboards, or about sadomasochism in computer games. All of these instances fall under the ill-defined regulatory concept of indecency. We cannot use a legal approach to arrive at a social solution—not if we want to remain true to the principles enshrined in the First Amendment.

"I shall not today attempt further to define [obscenity]," intoned Supreme Court justice Potter Stewart, famously adding, "but I know it when I see it."

Stewart has been roundly ridiculed for this sentiment over the four decades since he wrote it, in a concurring opinion overturning a ban on pornographic films. His comment seems to expose the utter subjectivity of obscenity prosecutions. But Stewart was really only stating that there may be a gulf between human language and human understanding. There are many times we know things that we cannot define.

I know it when I see it. A lot of us feel that way. Stewart was articulating a gruff, commonsense approach to obscenity. A court of law, with its endless shadings of meaning and language, can blur reality into nothingness. But an average person, looking at a downloaded photo from the Internet, has an immediate gut reaction. Such a visceral response ("I know it when I see it") might not have its place in the judicial process, but it surely counts for something in how we approach our social and cultural responsibilities.

PART FOUR

■ ■ ■

WHAT WE CAN DO

■ ■ ■

CHAPTER TWENTY-SIX

TELEVISION

I DON'T WANT TO LIVE IN a G-RATED WORLD. BUT I DO WANT TO LIVE in a V-chip world, a place where I can choose just what kinds of images are assaulting my eyeballs.

The V-chip, which is mandatory filtering hardware that today comes built into every television with picture screens of thirteen inches or larger, is a paradigm of end-user control of content. Rather than influence the broad spectrum of content on broadcast and cable, end-user control puts the choice back into the hands of the consumer. As our computers, televisions, and other appliances get ever "smarter," V-chip-style technology will be the most workable model for content control in the future.

Recall the radio and television sets of the past. They were the original electronic media devices. They were also "dumb," in the sense that they merely transferred whatever content came in over the airwaves, without respect to user taste. In contrast, newmodel DVDs, VCRs, and TVs are now "smart" in ways not imag-

ined just a few years ago. All these devices can work to help patrol personal boundaries of taste and decency so that individual
consumers become masters of their media domains.

The problem is that the V-chip may be too difficult to use. Or,
more to the point, it is not being used. Although V-chip technology is approaching the 50 percent level, at which time it will be
in half of all American homes, as of 2000 only about half of the
TV owners who had the V-chip were using it. Only about 10 percent of all parents can identify the age ratings of TV programs
that their children watch.

This is an education problem. Movie ratings have a higher rate
of familiarity with the public because they have been in use
longer. *Will and Grace* richly deserves its TV-14 rating (and it is
scheduled during erstwhile family hour despite this rating). But
if only a bare minority of viewers understands or uses the rating,
it does little good.

So understanding and using the V-chip is one clear step we
may take to regain control of the media content pumped into our
homes. But technology can never be the sole answer. TV programs need human eyes, to identify not just inappropriate sexual
content but worthy content also. We need monitors to judge
family-appropriate shows and bring them to our attention.

Luckily, there are some solid organizations that are doing just
that. Common Sense Media ("Sanity, Not Censorship") is the
most low-key of the advocacy groups, geared toward parents
sharing information with other parents.

Parents Television Council (PTC), for all its occasional over-the-topness, provides a superb online resource (www.parentstv. org) for recognizing what's right and wrong with the tube. One thing I like about it is that the Web site doesn't just carp. Every TV season as well as every week, there are "best show on television" choices that represent suitable and sometimes excellent family viewing.

Both these organizations help lobby broadcasters, cable TV companies, and entertainment conglomerates to act responsibly when it comes to programming. PTC's primary campaign is its push to reinstitute a kid-friendly family hour, beginning at eight o'clock every night. The networks paid brief lip service to the idea of a smut-free zone in prime time but began backsliding almost immediately.

The Coalition for Quality Children's Media publishes ratings for a lot more than just TV, and their Kids First! Web site (www.cqcm.org) is a bright, polemic-free resource with over three thousand reviews. The Lion and Lamb Project (www.lion-lamb.org) is oriented toward halting the marketing of violence to children.

Positive messages ("Here are the best shows to watch") are crucial. Any action that is seen as antitelevision is going to have only a limited impact, for a simple reason: Americans love their television. And "love" is not putting it too strongly. While the annual exercise of TV Turn-off Week (www.tvturnoff.org) is a good idea, it won't have any appreciable impact on viewing habits. There have been TV Turnoff Weeks every year for over a decade now, yet where do we find ourselves almost every evening?

Presently, ten companies own over 90 percent of the media outlets. Among entertainment providers, the picture is even more limited. Merger mania among vast multinational conglomerates has produced a top-heavy media universe, dominated in the United States by five corporations.

The five dominant companies represent fairly concise targets, just in case you feel like venting your ire about smut on television. In other words, you only have to write five letters, tug on five sleeves, convince five CEOs to act responsibly—and you will have addressed the vast majority of television programming choices in this country.

Time Warner is the biggest entertainment conglomerate in the world. Among its holdings are the WB Network, HBO, Cinemax, CNN, TBS, TNT, the Cartoon Network, and half ownership of Comedy Central. The company also has very active television production arms, including Warner Bros. studios, New Line, and HBO Independent Productions.

Next biggest behind Time Warner is Viacom, owner of CBS and producer (through its control of MTV) of the infamous Janet Jackson Super Bowl halftime show. Also in the Viacom stable are cable's most popular kids' network, Nickelodeon, and its spin-offs, as well as Showtime, VH1, and CMT. Infinity Broadcasting, soon to be the former home of Howard Stern, is a Viacom company.

Disney/ABC is the world's third largest media conglomerate, which not only controls the named network but also has ownership interests in a wide array of cable channels, such as ESPN, A&E, The History Channel, and Lifetime. Its production entities include Walt Disney Pictures, Miramax Films, and Hollywood Pictures.

The newly created NBC Universal was formed in the wake of a huge deal between a U.S. blue-chip, GE (the former General Electric) and the French entertainment giant Vivendi. Now the fourth big player in American media, NBC Universal controls Telemundo, USA Network, Sci-Fi Channel, Bravo, Trio, CNBC, and MSNBC, as well as NBC itself and Universal Studios. GE owns 80 percent of the conglomerate, with the remaining fifth still owned by Vivendi.

Finally, there is News Corporation, home of Fox, with subsidiaries that provide filmed entertainment, TV, cable, satellite TV, magazines, newspapers, and books. News Corporation includes such varied holdings as 20th Century Fox film studios, *TV Guide,* the FX cable channel, and HarperCollins book publishing.

Time Warner, Viacom, Disney, Universal, and Fox. These five companies control, own, produce, or program almost all of what is seen on our television screens. Corporate behemoths such as these change direction about as easily as an aircraft carrier, but with enough public pressure brought to bear, it can be done.

There is another way to look at it, too. There are five companies, but there are also five individuals, CEOs who control those companies. Five men who, whether they will own up to it or not, are responsible for what is on TV.

Richard Parsons of Time Warner. Sumner Redstone of Viacom. Michael Eisner (or whoever succeeds him) of Disney. Bob Wright of Universal. Rupert Murdoch of Fox.

That narrows it down even further, and makes the effort that much easier. We the public don't actually have to turn the air-craft carrier ourselves; all we have to do is convince the captain that it is in his best interest to do so.

If we want to change TV, we need to change the minds of these five men.

WHAT WE CAN DO: TELEVISION

- Understand and use V-chips, lockboxes, and other filtering devices.
- Consult and support organizations such as Common Sense Media, Parents Television Council, and Coalition for Quality Children's Media.
- Apply direct advocacy efforts to the CEOs of the Big Five media conglomerates.

CHAPTER TWENTY-SEVEN

■ ■ ■

THE INTERNET

NOTHING CAN BE DONE ABOUT ONLINE SEX. THE INTERNET IS
too complex, too sprawling, too out of control. It's global. It's decentralized. The cat's already out of the bag. I don't really even
understand the technology, and if I did, it wouldn't do any good,
because . . . well, because the Internet's too complex, too sprawling, too out of control.

That, anyway, is the accepted wisdom. The excuse used for
not doing anything about the stunning proliferation of smut online. Raise the white flag of defeat.

Part of this is simply the twentieth-century human's response
to twenty-first-century reality. Computers can induce a coma of
helplessness precisely because they are so complex. Whereas
with the internal combustion engine, say, the rational mind can
trace back cause and effect (the gas line's connected to the car-
buretor, the carb's connected to the manifold), with a computer
that's not possible. When our rational mind bumps up against

such an opaque, fiendishly intricate technology, it balks. High-tech anxiety and digital dread result.

But the Internet may be the single most tractable sector of our sex-drenched lives. The most oversexed area of our culture could be the one that is simplest to change. Because it is a digital world, changes may be applied instantaneously, or at least at the speed of light. As technology has betrayed us, bombarding people with smut whether they choose it or not, technology can also be part of the fix.

It's useful to think of the Internet as a whole lot of printing presses (personal computers) connected to a large number of bookstores (computer servers). In this metaphorical example, sexual content is everywhere, on many of the individual presses and in almost every bookstore.

But what if the owner of a printing press wishes not to be a publisher of smut? What if we want to preserve the privacy of our personal printing presses?

Being an unwilling pornographer sounds unlikely, but there is so much X-rated content zipping around the Net these days that some of it inevitably slops over onto personal computers. When you think about it, that's an outrageous transgression, especially if the victim is someone truly offended by smut. It's as though an intruder sneaked into your home and stole pen and paper to write up, say, hate flyers.

Luckily, we can lock our doors if we choose to. Using technology, we can block specific content so that our personal printing press prints only stuff that we choose. Filtering software has become ever more sophisticated, almost keeping up with the exploding growth of content and delivery systems. Almost, but not quite—filters will never be the only tool we need to assert our right to privacy, but they are important ones.

Say I want to keep all sexual content off my own private printing press. Yet the bookstores—the computer servers out there—are filled with smut. I could, of course, disconnect my printing press from the vast network of bookstores. No one is forcing me to go online. But that would deprive me of the enormous benefits of the Internet, all that great stuff out there that I would choose to access were it not intermixed with material I decidedly don't want.

So what do I do? Scour all the bookstores and remove all the material to which I object?

Apart from being fairly impossible, what with half the bookstores located halfway around the world, under the control of who-knows-what government, that approach doesn't make much sense. Besides, why should I be the one to choose what's in everyone's bookstores?

There's a much better, much more workable idea: to choose what kind of material is transferred from the bookstore/server to my printing press/personal computer. If we think of the vast amount of content as the large end of a funnel, it makes sense to control content at the small end, at its point of entry into the home.

This is the approach that holds the most promise in dealing with Internet smut. The end-user approach places choice in the hands of each and every one of us—where it should be. Computers, of course, are the original "smart" appliances, capable of handling sophisticated tasks of sorting and separating.

"Filters don't work." That's what you'll hear in response to any positive portrayal of the utility of filtering software. Some of that is the Chattering Class talking, the my-every-word-is-gold-I-can't-stand-the-thought-of-some-censor!-cen-SOR! class that is absolutely inflexible in this regard. Yes, filters do have problems with overblocking (shutting too much out) and underblocking (letting too much through). There is an inverse relation between the two problems: reducing overblocking increases underblocking, and vice versa.

But as an essential weapon in the battle to take back our computers, filters are a first line of defense. They can be combined with other end-user strategies. Spam filtering software, for example, is another end-user technology that is effective in stemming the tide of sexually explicit e-mails. Antispam technology resembles a digital genie who gets to the mailbox before you do and tosses out all the junk mail. Thanks, genie!

Computer monitoring software represents another approach, especially effective when a parent can't be in the room with a child every minute a computer is connected to the Internet. Such monitoring produces an audit trail of Internet use so that you can know in what kind of Web neighborhoods your kid hangs out. Does that smack of Big Brother? Well, yes, it does. One of the mournful realities of having children is that it does involve a measure of Big Brothering—also known as parenting.

Filters, monitors, and antispam programs all represent voluntary end-user tools that allow us to reassert choice, protect privacy, and regain control over what has become an essential and otherwise overwhelmingly positive component of modern life.

Did you catch that word "voluntary" in there? That means no government is mandating any of these measures. No laws require their use. Voluntary, as opposed to mandatory. I don't know how I can make it any clearer. Just so that the undies of the Chattering Class remain unbunched.

Internet service providers (ISPs) can also filter spam and sexual content, not at the end-user level, but at the server level. Some providers are more adept at doing this than others. Prodigy bills itself as the "family-friendly" ISP and has strict protocols about what sort of content gets pumped into your home.

There are other, tremendously promising ways in which technology can help make the Internet a realm of choice instead of coercion. Recent proposals for top-level domain names—these are Internet address tags like .com, .org. or .edu—include one designed to help end users filter out unwanted sexual material. The .xxx domain name would represent a catch-all realm where all adult content providers could hawk their wares, a digitally created sexual souk or red-light district that would have clearly marked borders. Abandon all modesty, ye who enter here.

No more blundering into adult-o-rama when your kid, doing homework research, innocently enters the word "beaver" into a search engine, since the search could be predicated on the domains your computer was programmed to search. No more misspelled URLs opening mousetrapped smut barrages, since it would be difficult to mistype "xxx" instead of "com." Porn would be effectively segregated but still readily available.

Again, a libertarian standard would preclude anything but a voluntary use of the top-level triple-x domain. So do we depend on the kindness of pornographers to make this strategy effective? In fact, there is some indication that adult-content providers would actually welcome an online "Combat Zone" (which is what they used to call the old Boston porn district) of their own. The president of one of the largest smut companies on the Internet said as much when he testified in front of a Senate committee in 1998.

But, all right, say voluntary compliance wasn't complete. There are always rogue outliers in any business. Say only 90 percent of adult content was safely relegated to the triple-x domain. The remaining 10 percent (still a massive amount of material) would resemble a flock of fat chickens, waiting to be plucked by eager obscenity prosecutors. Fat, nervous chickens. Eventually, almost all of them would willingly return to the coop.

Filtering and other end-use remedies, coupled with aggressive employment of such top-level domains as .xxx (or, on the flip side, another proposed domain, .kids, with only vetted content allowed) would go a tremendous distance in addressing problems so many users experience on the Internet. There is no magic wand (there is *never* any magic wand, worse luck), but a combination of these strategies would be the next best thing. The effect would be startling, clearly visible, like night and day.

But there is one more thing. The most effective weapon of all against the unwanted intrusion of smut into our private worlds is education. Teaching your child Internet safety is part of what it means to be a modern parent. To this end, many schools and libraries have instituted something called acceptable use policies governing behavior while online.

AUPs, as these formal agreements are universally called, represent a contract of common social responsibility, defining in detail what is acceptable and what is not acceptable while using a computer. AUPs should be in place as a condition of using of the Internet as a public resource in a public space.

It's not a bad idea for our home computers to have AUPs, too, formal or informal, but spelled out in unambiguous fashion. Teaching ourselves and teaching our children proper techniques of using the Internet is the single most important strategy we can employ to make it our online experience a blessing rather than a betrayal.

WHAT WE CAN DO: THE INTERNET

- Don't become overwhelmed by the amount of sexual content on the Internet, or by the technology involved.

- Understand and install filtering devices, antispam software, monitoring programs, and other end-user technology to protect your home environment.

- Understand and employ ISP-based filtering and antispam protocols, or switch to a family-friendly ISP.

- Advocate the immediate implementation of top-level domain names to segregate smut.

- Implement a formal or informal acceptable use policy for your family.

■ ■ ■

CHAPTER TWENTY-EIGHT

THE PUBLIC COMMONS

AMONG THE MOST POPULAR TYPES OF COMPUTER GAMES ARE simulation games, such as Sim City, in which players don't compete against one another so much as play God, each player creating a whole imaginary world from scratch. Buildings, towns, economies flower and develop under the watchful prodding of the omnipotent human at the keyboard.

If we could indulge ourselves in playing simulation games in the real world, what kind of place would we create? The only reasonable kind of world to work toward is one in which we all can feel safe, comfortable, and at home.

Jangly, discordant, and sex-fevered, modern culture is most definitely not such a world. The aggressively sexual atmosphere of so many of our public spaces, be they real or virtual, is patently offensive to huge sectors of the populace. In fact, it is deliberately designed to be offensive. Is this any way to run a simulation game?

At one point during his reign, China's dictator Mao Tse-tung was gripped by a brief delusion that it might be a good idea to allow dissent. "Let a hundred flowers bloom, let a hundred schools of thought contend," he intoned, meaning that all different voices should be heard. Of course, when artists and intellectuals spoke up and criticized Mao and the Communist regime, the Great Leader had a swift change of mind. Dissenters were tossed in jail and the whole "hundred flowers" initiative was nipped in the bud.

In American culture we very much want a hundred flowers blooming—a thousand flowers, a million. We want to provide the most expansive arena for people to think, talk, and operate, and we are willing to give up some level of comfort to be able to accomplish this.

So any simulation that we dream up has to accommodate as many flowers as possible. We can't eliminate speech, since eliminating speech means eliminating ideas. But gardens have borders. We can set boundaries and create filters—behind which those who are uncomfortable with overtly sexual speech may still feel at home in our world.

Imagine a sprawling central area in our simulation game. This public commons is large and gracious, tree-lined and open. Above all, it is kid-welcoming, a place where young children can play, grow, and thrive. It is a place where those among us who have strong religious prohibitions against overt sexual display are at ease. If people chose, they could live out their whole lives and never leave the public commons.

But let's venture out of the commons for a moment. There are streets leading off, broad avenues branching away into the distance, and alleyways leading off of them, in intricate webs of habitation and enterprise. Here and there are rooms or courtyards, out of sight of the public commons, where every possible human endeavor, ambition, activity, and idea may be explored.

Yes, many of these activities may be sexual, but they are not splayed out across the public commons. Constructs of gross and deliberate offensiveness might be eschewed out of choice, out of recognition they arise from feelings of social insecurity. No one's face is rubbed in the sexual, the nasty, the distasteful, simply because this or that vulgarian needs to act out.

Here is the kind of culture toward which we need to strive. No legal mandate will do it, but it requires a recognition that this is the best way for human beings to live. Especially in a screamingly diverse society such as ours, we need to be guardians of each other's feelings.

I'm with Hannibal Lecter: I consider rudeness to be one of the cardinal human sins. And American popular culture, as we've constructed it here at the beginning of the millennium, is above all else rude, crude and lewd.

Like the two main electronic versions of the public commons, television and the Internet, our physical public commons—the public space we inhabit and pass through every day—is afflicted by an onslaught of sex. The difference is in public, sexual representations are non-disengageable. We may be able to filter content on TV or the Web, but unless we decide to be hermits we can't shut off this assault on our public spaces.

The public commons requires a G rating on all forms of display. In fashion, on magazine covers, and on billboards, indecent sexual content intrudes into our lives whether we choose it or not.

There are voluntary ways to stop this from happening. Retailers can provide a whole spectrum of fashions, instead of just one kind. Magazine publishers can put anything they want on their covers, but in public display sexual content needs to be masked or shrink-wrapped. And billboard companies must operate on a strict G-rated-content-only policy.

This all might sound like a utopian dream, given the current state of display in our public commons. But small efforts by ordinary people have paid off big dividends in precisely this area.

"Dear Nordstrom," wrote a Washington-state girl named Ellen Gunderson in a letter to chain-store clothing retailer, "I'm an 11-year-old girl who has tried shopping at your store for clothes, in particular jeans. But all of them ride way under my hips and the next size up is too big and it falls down. Your clerk suggests there is only one 'look.' If that is true then girls are supposed to walk around half naked. I think we need to change that."

Surprisingly, the company responded, increasing the variety of its clothing offerings. Other retail chains have been convinced in much the same way, by direct pressure from community groups. And all these individual efforts might be paying off with an industry-wide shift.

"Prim Is In!" declared one recent report on fashion trends, which quoted one fashionista's withering observation, "Baring your bellybutton is so 90s."

In Las Vegas, the Battle of the Billboards is an ongoing fight, one that hasn't yet been resolved. In 2004 the Nevada Gaming

Commission and the Hard Rock Hotel and Casino came to an agreement over a disputed sign (not the "Buck All Night" one, but one that showed a man and woman splayed out on a black-jack table with the line "There's always a temptation to cheat"), with the Hard Rock agreeing to pay a whopping three-hundred-thousand-dollar fine for presenting the gaming industry in a bad light.

That agreement, though, was tossed out, partially in response to a determined group of citizen activists, who've formed organizations like the Main Street Billboard Committee, the Nevada Chapter of American Mothers Inc., Nevada Concerned Citizens, and Porn Only In Zone (POIZ), among others.

The groups lobbied to have the billboards cleaned up, not of their references to cheating at cards, but of their sexual imagery. The agreement with Hard Rock did not go far enough, and did not address sexual content at all. Billboards, because everyone can see them—adults and children, prudes and libertines, and, in Las Vegas, residents and tourists—need to be G rated.

During this citizen-advocacy effort, it became clear that these folks don't want to bring down the gaming industry. They know that gambling brings in the revenue that allows them to live without a state income tax. They know that the thirty-two million tourists who visit Las Vegas every year underwrite the city's schools, streets, infrastructure.

But their message is a lot like the message of this book: keep sexual imagery where it belongs.

"It's a city of choices, and as a general rule of thumb, I don't want somebody choosing what's right for me and my family,"

Michael Wixom of Las Vegas's Main Street Billboard Committee told reporters. "I can't choose when it's on a billboard. I can turn off the TV, but I can't turn off a billboard."

We can't turn off someone else's radio, either, so at least to some extent radio falls under the domain of our physical public commons. Luckily, the issue of smut on the radio might solve itself. Bubba the Love Sponge was fired. Howard Stern was chased from the public airwaves and will set up shop on the subscription-only Sirius satellite network. Eminem has mentioned going this route, too.

That is, in fact, what this book is all about. Talk about anal sex all you want, prattle about masturbation or rap about fellatio. It's a free country. But don't do it on the public dime, over the public airwaves, in the public commons. Take it private, as Stern has done.

This would be a consummation devoutly to be wished, since it would allow those who want to hear these geniuses ample opportunity to do so, while sparing the rest of us anal sex talk in the early a.m. The public commons would be the better for it.

I've talked a lot in this book about my experiences working in adult magazines. My personal situation is relevant only because it looks as though we are enshrining smut as a central part of our culture. We're working toward giving it pride of place in our public commons, and I don't believe that's healthy, necessary, or bright. In fact, it's a form of civic laziness.

Smut has somehow gained status as the primary vehicle for our sexuality. It has become the most common way for adolescents to be introduced to sex—and not via the soft-core airbrushed nudity of *Playboy*, either, but via the aggressive, raw-edged sexuality of the Internet.

"A widespread taste for pornography," says the writer J. G. Ballard, probably putting too much thought into it, "means that nature is alerting us to some threat of extinction."

The subtitle of this book portrays me as a "concerned father," and I certainly am that. But I'm a concerned human being, too. Even a cursory survey of the media landscape, such as the one this book attempts, reveals a world so clearly out of balance that the final effect is dizzying—and nauseating.

We need a voluntary effort to reshape our culture. It's that simple, and that difficult. We need to do this for our children, yes, but we also need to accomplish this for ourselves.

WHAT WE CAN DO: THE PUBLIC COMMONS

- Insist on voluntary G-rated display policies for local signage companies and newsstands.
- Support safety efforts to ban visual display of X-rated material on vehicle DVD screens.
- Search out and support fashion companies that don't use sexually aggressive advertising or pander to teenage taste for inappropriate clothing.
- Oppose legally mandated censorship, but maintain a strong advocacy for voluntary boundaries on indecency, resisting Chattering Class efforts to mischaracterize those boundaries as censorship.

ACKNOWLEDGMENTS

THIS BOOK WOULD NOT HAVE BEEN WRITTEN BUT FOR THE interest, encouragement, and commitment of two people, my editor Bernadette Malone at Sentinel and my agent, Paul Bresnick. In an arena of political opposites, we found common ground. Thanks to Peter B. for making the connection. Several of my friends gave me support, including Peter Z., Betsy, and Barbara, and the first two names listed in the dedication. Many more of my friends argued vociferously against this project, and for that I'd like to thank them, too, since their opposition was a deciding factor in my embarking on it. My wife, Jean Zimmerman, is as always a writer's dream as first editor, sounding board, and all-around helpmate. Other members of my family were there for me in ways that are constantly rejuvenating. They know that however a dedication reads, I do it all for them.

■ ■ ■

Footnotes and a select bibliography may be found at
www.smutthebook.com.

INDEX